HAUNTED STARK COUNTY

HAUNTED STARK COUNTY

A GHOULISH HISTORY

SHERRI BRAKE

Haunted
America

Published by Haunted America
A Division of The History Press
Charleston, SC 29403
www.historypress.net

Copyright © 2009 by Sherri Brake
All rights reserved

First published 2009
Second printing 2011
Third printing 2012
Fourth printing 2013

ISBN 9781540219534

Library of Congress Cataloging-in-Publication Data

Brake, Sherri.
Haunted Stark County : a ghoulish history / Sherri Brake.
p. cm.
ISBN 9781540219534
1. Haunted places--Ohio--Stark County--History--Anecdotes. 2. Ghosts--
Ohio--Stark County--History--Anecdotes. 3. Stark County (Ohio)--History--
Anecdotes. 4. Stark County (Ohio)--History, Local--Anecdotes. I. Title.
BF1472.U6B695 2009
133.109771'62--dc22
2009013737

CONTENTS

FOREWORD

Ohio's history is a fascinating one, an exciting pageant that mirrors much of American history. It is a tale of ancient Native American Mound Builders and the many native nations— such as the Shawnees and Miamis—that followed them. It is a tale of venturesome European settlers crossing the Appalachian Mountains to carve out new settlements in the wilderness. Both the French and Indian War and the American Revolution were fought in the wild frontier of the Ohio country. The state's history also includes stories about the multitudes of Irish immigrants who hand-dug thousands of miles of canals throughout the state in the nineteenth century and the daring slaves who escaped to freedom from the Civil War South by way of Ohio's Underground Railroad. The history also includes Prohibition-era bootleggers and gangsters and so much more.

Stark County in northeastern Ohio has played an important role in Ohio's dramatic story. It has witnessed Ohio's history from the original Native Americans right up to modern times, and all those people, over so many years, have left their marks on the state. In fact, it's possible that many of them remain among us today. You see, Stark County is haunted.

Sherri Brake has lived for many years in the little Stark County town of Canal Fulton. Sherri is, to say the least, a complex woman—a mother, a Civil War reenactor, a historian and a ghost hunter. The last two attributes in particular are what make her the perfect author for this book.

I first met Sherri in 2003, when I was researching my book *Ghosthunting Ohio* (Emmis Books, 2004). She answered my Internet request for information about haunted locations in Ohio and provided me with a list of places in her part of the state. I drove to Canal Fulton, where I met with Sherri. She introduced me to the haunted warehouse on the canal and showed me the canal locks and a section of the old canal that still exists in Canal Fulton. In the town's Pioneer Cemetery, Sherri taught me how to dowse.

We stood in the snowy cemetery on a winter's day, just as the sun began to slip below the horizon. Using metal dowsing rods that she had made herself, she showed me not only how to dowse for buried objects and fields of energy but also how to determine the gender of people buried in the cemetery. Sherri would stand alongside a grave, one dowsing rod in her hand. As she explained to me, if the rod pointed toward the head of the grave a woman was buried there. If it pointed toward the foot of the grave, it was a man. I asked her why that was, and she replied that it was because women thought with their brains and men thought with an organ located considerably lower than the brain. With a sense of humor like that, I knew we would be friends.

Sherri has investigated many haunted locations in Stark County and also throughout Ohio and West Virginia. Her method is balanced and rational, as she is neither a wide-eyed ghost fanatic nor a skeptic. Hers is an inquiring mind, seeking to explain what seems to be unexplainable. In addition to her investigations, Sherri conducts several ghost tours, including tours to the Mansfield Reformatory and Zoar Village, both in Ohio, and West Virginia's Moundsville State Penitentiary.

Over the last several years, I have been a guest on some of Sherri's haunted tours, and I have featured her in both my books *Ghosthunting Ohio* and *Ghosthunters: On the Trail of Mediums, Dowsers, Spirit Seekers and Other Investigators of America's Paranormal World* (New Page Books, 2007). Together, we have conducted investigations of haunted locations, as well as "Ghosthunting 101" classes open to the general public. She is, to my mind, the epitome of what a good ghost hunter should be.

FOREWORD

When it comes to local history, and especially haunted history, Sherri is one of the most knowledgeable people I know. Informative and entertaining, she's a born storyteller. I am certain that you will enjoy reading this book.

John B. Kachuba
Cincinnati, Ohio
www.JohnKachuba.com

PREFACE

U pon embarking on this project, I knew I had several goals. First and foremost, I wanted to share with readers my love for the history of the area known as Stark County, Ohio. Secondly, I wanted to help readers explore outside the box of your typical "textbook history." In other words, what you will find between the covers of this book may surprise you a bit. There are some tidbits of history amongst these pages that have been buried for many years. It's the darker side of history, the type you never seem to learn in school, yet for many people, including myself, it's the history that we seem to remember the most—the frontier slayings, the Indian battles, the lynchings, the gangster shootouts, the ghost stories and the cemetery folklore. This is the common thread that ties this foray into haunted history together. My third goal was to include a look into one of the nation's fastest-growing hobbies: the paranormal and the subject of investigating ghosts.

This book is just another way to spark interest in what is *local* for both adults and children. Our local history. Our historical buildings and towns. Our scenic canals and rivers. They are all things that we usually see on a daily basis, but they are so much more than that. Nearly every old house, field, parking lot or building has a tale to tell. Sometimes you just need to take the time to listen and research. Is every place haunted? No. But I can guarantee that a stroll through any neighborhood locally will yield stories of odd things in homes that are unexplained. I have personally investigated hundreds of homes and businesses in Stark County alone. There have been allotments built over Native American burial grounds, houses built over cemeteries supposedly moved years ago, businesses where staff and customers experience things—and the list goes on and on. I have worked with land developers, park managers and cemetery associations in finding unmarked burials. I have investigated haunted rentals, haunted stores and even a haunted factory. I have worked with private homeowners who have possible hauntings. What you will find here in *Haunted Stark County* is a sampling of what this county holds in its history and hauntings.

I hope you find this book to be entertaining, enlightening and a bit educational. Welcome to the world of haunted history!

ACKNOWLEDGEMENTS

With any project, there are people to thank for their support, interest and encouragement. First and foremost, I thank my family for their support and encouragement through the writing and gathering of information for *Haunted Stark County*. Thank you to my parents, Larry and Suzi Brake, who let me entertain my love for ghost stories, vampire movies and the paranormal since I was a small child without suggesting I go to therapy; to my sisters Terri and Shawni, for their encouragement and for both being normal and letting me be the "odd" one; to my children, Sage and Mason Recco, for letting Mommy venture into dark haunted buildings and creepy cemeteries without being overly concerned; to my second-grade teacher, Miss Bonnie Tewanger, for encouraging my love of reading, which opened up a whole new world for me; and to the many ghost hunters and paranormal groups in the state of Ohio and beyond who have supported this book and what it is all about. Special thanks to Angel Reader Laura Wissler, who is a true friend and fellow investigator. Thank you to Brian Fain of the Massillon Ghost Hunters Society for all of his great ideas and friendly encouragement; to author John Kachuba for his friendship and for including me in a couple of his great books on the paranormal; and to the directors, staff and awesome volunteers of the Mansfield Reformatory, the West Virginia State Penitentiary, the Rogues Hollow Historical Society, the Massillon cemetery and the Ohio Historical Society for permitting us to have great events at their sites over the last five years. Hugs to the many folks who have become part of the Haunted Heartland Tour family and continue to do events and hunts with us. Last but not least, I offer unending gratitude to Perry for his encouragement and support when I needed it the most.

I hope you find this book intriguing, and perhaps it will have you looking at locations around the county in a different light. History ain't always pretty!

STARK COUNTY, OHIO

The Start of Stark

Early settlers in the area now known as Stark County, Ohio, were greeted by Native Americans when they first arrived during the great westward movement. The frontier of Ohio was a vast wilderness, and when the white settlers came upon it, they worked hard and fast to settle and change the landscape. In 1799, they signed a treaty with various local tribes that allowed the area to be surveyed and settled. The rolling terrain of the county had been home to various wildlife, and the rivers and lakes were plentiful with fish and ran deep and clear with that most precious commodity known as fresh water. Settlers here in Stark County tamed the wilderness, built cabins, grew crops and hunted game as they left their mark on the ever-changing landscape.

Stark County is situated in the northeast section of Ohio and was originally part of Columbiana County. Canton, which is the county seat, lies in the forks of the Nimishillen River, a tributary of the Muskingum River. The county area, in square miles, totals 567, and the elevation ranges from 880 feet in the southeast corner of Bethlehem Township to 1,360 feet above sea level near the northern part of the town of Paris. Some twenty thousand years ago, a glacier that covered most of North America forged a line through the middle of the county. The county sits on what is referred to as the unglaciated Allegheny Plateau. In prehistoric days, the earliest settlers and explorers were Mound Builders. After 1750, the Delaware tribe established a small

An 1870s geological map of Ohio. *Courtesy of the Ohio Historical Society.*

village just a few miles south of the southern border of Stark County, near the present-day town of Bolivar. This town was a capital for the Delaware tribe and was called Tuscarawas Town. The word *Tuscarawas* is popular in the Stark County area and is said to mean "Open Mouth" in the Delaware language. At the time of European contact, and in the years that followed,

A Ghoulish History

General John Stark.
Courtesy of the Heritage Center Collection.

Native Americans in the current territory of Ohio included the Shawnees, Iroquois, Miamis and Wyandots.

Stark County derives its name from Revolutionary War soldier General John Stark. General Stark was the oldest surviving Revolutionary War general before his death in 1822. He became widely known as the "Hero of Bennington" for his exemplary service at the Battle of Bennington in 1777. General Stark seems to be more of a New Hampshire hero than one recognized in the county named for him. His statue stands before the state capitol in New Hampshire and his legend looms large. Tradition says that he coined the famous Granite State motto "Live free or die." General John Stark and his wife, Molly, never traveled west of Buffalo, New York, but their son Caleb owned land in Tuscarawas County, Ohio, and points farther south in the Buckeye State. Of the eleven children blessed to the union of John and Molly Stark, Caleb was the only one to venture into Ohio. During the war, Molly Stark often tended to the sick and dying troops in New Hampshire, and when a tuberculosis sanatorium was built in Stark County, it was named after her. Molly Stark Hospital stood near Alliance, Ohio, and several buildings remain as of the writing of this book. Molly

17

Stark died of typhus in 1814 at age seventy-eight. John was eighty-six at the time. He lived into his ninety-fourth year and died on May 8, 1822.

But who were the first human inhabitants in what is now Ohio? The Mound Builders occupied parts of Ohio and the Ohio River Valley during the Woodland period. During this time, there were two groups of prehistoric people, the Hopewells and the Adenas. The most famous mound in the state of Ohio is the Serpent Mound in Adams County. It is 1,330 feet in length along its coils and averages three feet in height. The Adena culture refers to the prehistoric American Indian peoples who lived in southern Ohio and neighboring regions of West Virginia, Kentucky and Indiana during the early Woodland period. They were the first people in this region to settle down in small villages, cultivate crops, use pottery as a vessel, acquire exotic raw materials (such as copper and shell) to make ornaments and jewelry and bury their honored dead in conical burial mounds.

As for the early European settlers, the earliest known white settler in Stark County was a Moravian missionary by the name of

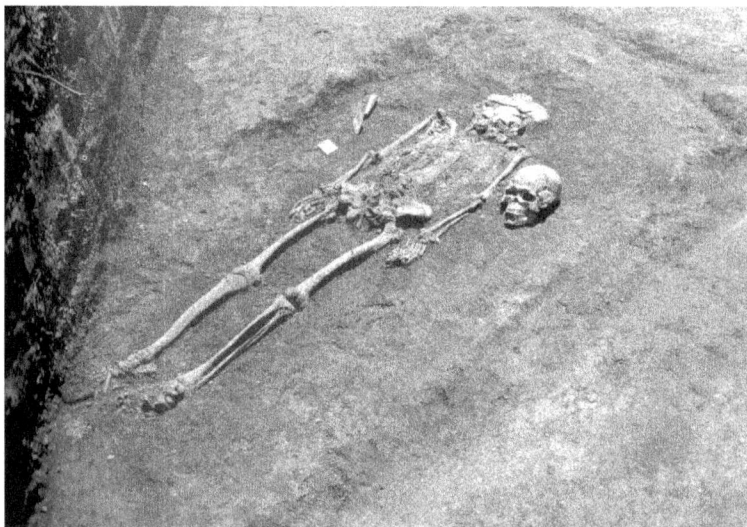

A Hopewell burial with a "trophy" skull. *Courtesy of the Ohio Historical Society.*

A Ghoulish History

The signing of the Treaty of Greenville, 1795. *Courtesy of the Ohio Historical Society.*

Christian Frederick Post. Post carved a piece of workable property from the wilderness in Bethlehem Township and built a cabin in 1761. Continental Congress passed a land ordinance in 1785 that ordered surveys in the eastern part of Ohio, in the area known as the Congress Lands. In 1795, the Treaty of Greenville opened up most of the area now known as Ohio to settlement. This treaty also pushed the remaining Native Americans west of the Tuscarawas River. On February 19, 1803, President Jefferson signed an act of Congress that approved Ohio's boundaries and constitution.

One interesting historical marker in the county is a large boulder sitting near Erie Street in the Crystal Springs area. This large boulder was placed on the historical boundary line, commemorating a pact known as the Fort McIntosh Treaty between the Native Americans and the United States in 1785. The tribal leaders involved all agreed that they lived under the American government and could not form alliances with any other powers. They were to relinquish their lands in southern and eastern Ohio to the United States government. The tribes were confined to the western corner of what is now the state of Ohio, with an eastern border roughly running along the Cuyahoga River. The southern border extended from modern-day Akron westward toward the Tuscarawas River, south to Fort Laurens and west again toward Pickawillany on the Miami River. The western border ran north from Pickawillany to the St. Mary's River and then to what is now Fort Wayne, Indiana. A northern border from Fort Wayne to Lake Erie followed the shore of the lake east to the Cuyahoga River.

The boulder sits next to the Tuscarawas River and the Ohio & Erie Canal and pays tribute to the treaty between the Wyandot, Delaware, Chippewa and Ottawa Indians. It also denoted the line between the settlers and Indian Territory. All land west of this spot was Indian territory and all land east was U.S. territory. On this boulder is a bronze plaque that was placed in 1926 by the local Boy Scouts of America. Speeches were given and a band played music on the day of the unveiling, September 8, 1926. What many people do not know is that this boulder has a place in Indian lore and legend. It is said that this is a Spirit Stone and

Reverend David Zeisberger preaching to the Indians. *Painting by Christian Schuessle.*

that on nights when the sky is blessed with a full moon, the great stone begins to rock slightly back and forth in the darkness. The Spirit Stone is said to be mourning for the plight of the Native Americans many years ago.

The history of Stark County encompasses many eras, from frontier founding, growth and industry to suburban and city development. Early schools and churches became the cornerstone of many communities in the county, which features various landscapes, including small towns reminiscent of a Rockwell painting and urban downtown areas thriving with renovations. Drive across the county and you will see rolling farms, industrial sites, wooded acreage and suburban sprawl. Municipalities of this county include Alliance, Beach City, Brewster, Canal Fulton, Canton, East Canton, East Sparta, Hartville, Hills and Dales, Limaville, Louisville, Magnolia, Massillon, Meyers Lake, Minerva, Navarre, North Canton, Waynesburg and Wilmot. Townships include Bethlehem, Canton, Jackson, Lake, Lawrence, Lexington, Marlboro, Nimishillen, Osnaburg, Paris, Perry, Pike, Plain, Sandy, Sugar Creek, Tuscarawas and Washington. Other localities include Greentown, Maximo, Middlebranch, North Lawrence, Paris, Perry Heights, Robertsville and Uniontown.

Bezaleel Wells, Canton's founder, formerly owned the land on which the city of Steubenville, Ohio, is built. Mr. Wells was born in Baltimore County, Maryland, in the year 1769 and founded Canton in 1805. By occupation he was a farmer and miller, and he also possessed knowledge of civil engineering, having done much government surveying in both Maryland and Pennsylvania.

The Canton community grew slowly during the first half of the nineteenth century. By 1815, only three hundred people resided in the town. One of the main reasons for Canton's slow development was said to be its distance from main transportation routes. During the late 1820s, planners and developers of the Ohio & Erie Canal offered to build the canal through Canton. Residents refused to allow it, believing that disease would run rampant due to the standing water in the canal. As a result, the Ohio & Erie Canal skipped over Canton, traveling through nearby Massillon, Ohio, instead. The canal actually improved the health of Massillon residents, as well as their finances, by draining the neighboring swamps of putrid standing water. Canton also rejected railroads initially. The developers of the Cleveland & Pittsburgh Railroad offered to build the track through Canton, but only if residents pledged $10,000 to the line's construction. City officials refused because they believed that the railroad would have to build the track through Canton anyway. The developers constructed the line eighteen miles east of Canton, through Alliance, allowing Alliance to prosper and develop.

To speak of Canton and not mention sports and their development locally would be remiss. In 1920, local organizers founded the first professional football league in the city. In honor of this historical event, the National Football League authorized the Hall of Fame to be located in the city of Canton. The Professional Football Hall of Fame continues to be a main draw for local tourists and visitors in Stark County.

Downtown Canton, 1867. *Courtesy of Don Myers.*

A Ghoulish History

With the arrival of main roads, canals and the railroad, this area boomed and grew in both industry and population. To give the reader an idea of the county's growth in population from 1820 through 1880, consider the following:

YEAR	POPULATION
1820	12,406
1830	26,552
1840	34,617
1860	42,978
1880	64,031

Stark County had become a center of industry and continued to do so into the nineteenth and twentieth centuries, with companies such as Diebold's, the Timken Company, the Hoover Company, Dueber-Hampden Clockworks and Republic Steel, to name just a few.

Stark County became a destination for travelers, and many of those travelers decided to stay. With the arrival of the early immigrants, Stark County truly was a melting pot of ethnicities. When they settled in the area, the immigrants brought with them their lifestyles, which consisted of, among other things, music, stories, superstitions and religious beliefs. Many of these can still be sampled today across the county. The early immigrants built churches, schools, homes, roads and, later, railroads. The Ohio & Erie Canal opened up Ohio to both trade and travel. Stark County's geographical position between the Allegheny Mountains and the Mississippi River and Great Lakes ensured its suitability for growth and homesteading. It truly was an important part of Ohio and the growing nation as well.

LIFE ON THE FRONTIER

The Settlers' Superstitions and Omens

Pioneer and frontier living in Ohio was simply a life or death situation. Death was experienced by many at an early age, and many dealt with it on a daily basis. The manner of living for the pioneers, who made their homes at the forward edge of United States settlement as the frontier moved westward, was wrought with superstition, religious beliefs and the desire to survive. The primary lure of the Ohio frontier for the settler was land, either free or at a low price. It is generally agreed that by 1890 the frontier had come to an end.

On the frontier, a homesite was ideally constructed near a spring and, if the area was partly settled, near other pioneers or a fort (often called a station). Water was a precious commodity. If it could not be found in a lake, pond or stream, dowsing rods were sometimes used, or a water witcher helped the family find a suitable spot for a well. The first shelter—unless the family was living temporarily on the boat that brought them downriver or at the fort—was a rough shed of stacked logs, open across the front. This was called a half-faced camp. The pioneer family began at once to cut down trees for a log cabin. When enough had been cut, neighbors came to the log, or cabin, rising to help build the cabin.

Generally, three days were required to complete a cabin and its essential pieces of furniture—a platform bed built into a corner, a table and a few benches and stools. Logs and half logs, called puncheons, were used wherever possible because they were easier to make than hand-split planks. The cabin floor might be of puncheons, but more often it was packed dirt. The fireplace, built of logs and lined with stones and mud, was at one end of the room. It served for both heating and cooking. The cabin had a loft, reached by a ladder, where the children would sleep. The first building in Canton was a small log cabin on the east side of Market Street North. It was built by Garret Crusen in 1806.

John Bowers built a cabin in Stark County in 1806 in Nimishillen Township, on a hill west of Nimishillen Creek. John was a county commissioner and tax collector and traveled the county from home to home doing his job. Later in 1806, the Bowers family lost a child in the hard Ohio winter. The little boy fell victim to a fever and was placed in a crude and simple coffin made out of an old wagon box. The boy's grave was dug quickly, and the body was laid to rest in the woods near the cabin on the hill. A tree was felled and laid across the grave to keep the ever-curious wolves from destroying his final resting place.

Simply stated, people on the frontier banded together for work and often to celebrate a birth or mourn a death. Simple times these were, but they were also times when people embraced great fears

John Bowers and his cabin, built in 1806. *Courtesy of the Louisville Public Library Collection.*

or superstitions of the unknown. These frontier people believed in planting by the signs. Planting by the signs is still in practice in many rural communities, most of which are in the South. For the frontiersman and people who use this method, planting by the signs is a fairly straightforward operation. Through tradition, many frontier folks accepted the signs as the proper way to plant and harvest their crops. Based on the ancient astronomers' recognition of the Zodiac, the twelve signs come around every twenty-eight days and are divided into elements (fire, earth, air and water) and body parts (head, neck, breast, bowels, loins, knees, feet, legs, thighs, kidneys, heart and arms). Using a calendar or almanac that delineates the days of the month by signs, a farmer would pick the series of days with the most favorable signs for planting or harvesting his crops. In addition, many believe that the best time to plant crops with yields aboveground is while the moon is waxing and those with yields below ground (root crops like potatoes, radishes, peanuts, etc.) while the moon is waning. There are many other rules for planting, harvesting, plowing, transplanting and even cutting timber, romancing, hunting, cooking or cutting your hair. If a farmer did not heed the moon sign and planted against it, his crops would not fare well.

The settlers here in Ohio saw the world as a delicate balance, with spirits of good and evil in proximity. This balance extended beyond the spiritual world—they believed that the laws of nature were similarly related and that changes that made things more appealing would also make them more healthful. In times of plague and disease, they burned scented firewood in the streets, and people carried sweet-smelling flowers in their pockets to ward off disease. The old children's nursery rhyme "Ring around the rosey. / A pocketful of posies. / Ashes, ashes. / We all fall down!" is a remnant of plague times and is an example of carrying sweet flowers to stave off disease and the smell of the dead.

Superstitions that made their way into Ohio and Stark County came from Germany, Ireland, England and Scotland, for the most part. Some of the superstitions are common ones that we take for granted even today. Fear of Friday the Thirteenth goes back thousands of years. There is a biblical reference to the unlucky

A fourteenth-century sketch of a death scene. *Courtesy of the Kim Jones Collection.*

number thirteen. Judas, the apostle who betrayed Jesus, was the thirteenth guest at the Last Supper. Both Friday and the number thirteen were once closely associated with capital punishment. In British tradition, Friday was the conventional day for public hangings, and there were supposedly thirteen steps leading up to the noose. More than 80 percent of high-rises lack a thirteenth floor. Many airports skip the thirteenth gate. Italians omit the number thirteen from their national lottery. In ancient Rome, witches reportedly gathered in groups of twelve; the thirteenth was believed to be the devil. If you have thirteen letters in your name, you will have the devil's luck. Jack the Ripper, Charles Manson, Jeffrey Dahmer, Theodore Bundy and Albert De Salvo all have thirteen letters in their names. It is traditionally believed that Eve tempted Adam with the apple on a Friday. Tradition also has it that the flood in the Bible, the confusion at the Tower of Babel and the death of Jesus Christ all took place on Friday. Many triskaidekaphobes, as those who fear the unlucky integer are known, point to the ill-fated mission to the moon, Apollo 13. Numerologists consider twelve a "complete" number. There are twelve months in a year, twelve signs of the zodiac, twelve gods of Olympus, twelve labors of Hercules, twelve tribes of Israel and twelve apostles of Jesus. In exceeding twelve by one, thirteen's association with bad luck has to do with just being a little beyond completeness or normality. Thirteen is the sixth prime number, with six being considered unlucky due to its association with "666." Thirteen was an inconvenient number and, over time, acquired a reputation of evil that was reflected in such customs as tying a hangman's noose with thirteen loops. Other superstitions, including walking under ladders, breaking a mirror or looking glass, black cats, spilling salt or milk and even stepping on a sidewalk crack, hearken back to days in the old country.

Telling the future could be done in various ways on the Ohio frontier. The counting of crows was sometimes employed. One crow meant bad luck, two were lucky, three were good for health, four meant wealth, five meant sickness was coming and six meant death would appear. Some settlers carried acorns to bring luck and ensure long lives. Plants could also help foretell the future. Young pioneers would pick dandelions that had gone to seed and then take a deep breath and blow the seeds into the wind. They would count the seeds that remained on the stem, and the total would represent the number of children they would have. Another fortunetelling tradition involved the first flower of spring: the day a person found the first flower of the season could be used as an omen. Monday meant good fortune, Tuesday meant great attempts would be successful, Wednesday meant marriage, Thursday meant a warning of small profits, Friday meant wealth, Saturday meant misfortune and Sunday meant excellent luck for weeks.

There are common habits we all have today that we use sometimes without even thinking. Someone sneezes and many nearby will automatically respond with a hearty "Bless you!" When we react to that sneeze with a blessing, we are continuing a superstition that is hundreds, perhaps thousands, of years old. It was believed that when your mouth opened with a yawn or a sneeze, evil spirits could enter your body through your open mouth. Saying "Bless you!" was

An early Canton street scene. *Courtesy of Don Myers.*

a way to hopefully prevent the little demons from slipping down your throat, as was covering your mouth while yawning.

In early pioneer days, even doctors of medicine had little scientific knowledge. Canton's first doctor was Andrew Rappee, who moved to Canton in 1808. On the frontier, where doctors were unavailable, home remedies were frequently based on superstition and trial and error. For example, carrying a horse chestnut was thought to discourage rheumatism, and hanging a bag of asafetida (a vile-smelling resin exuded by certain plants) around a child's neck was believed to keep disease away. Hanging wolf's fangs around a child's neck was thought to keep them strong and healthy as well.

Herbs, roots, barks and berries were used for medicinal brews and extracts in the apparent belief that the stronger they tasted and smelled, the more effective they would be. Sassafras tea was drunk in the spring with the belief that it would thin the blood, a condition thought to be desirable for summer. Sulfur and molasses formed a spring tonic believed to purify the blood. Onion syrup was considered good for colds, coughs and the flu.

A Ghoulish History

Some folk remedies were found, later, to have real value. A poultice of moldy bread and water often was applied to an abscess. The mold on bread, it has since been discovered, contains the antibiotic known as penicillin. Foxglove, in the frontier days, was used to help heart conditions. It is now a main ingredient in the popular cardiac drug digoxin, which is widely used in the treatment of various heart conditions, namely atrial fibrillation and atrial flutter.

Superstitions and omens included the use of common items. An omen is anything perceived or happening that is believed to portend a good or evil event or circumstance in the future. Before using a loaf of bread, the sign of the cross was to be cut into it for good luck. This is where the term *hot cross buns* originates. There were many superstitions regarding brooms: never lean a broom against a bed or the evil spirits will cast a spell on the bed; never take a broom with you when you move or bad luck will follow; always buy a new broom. It was considered bad luck to leave a house using a different door than the one through which you entered. The same was said about getting up on the wrong side of the bed—one should always get in and get out on the same side. How often have you heard the phrase today "I got up on the wrong side of the bed!" Another common superstition thought to bring good luck was the practice of hanging horseshoes above the doorway. In most of Europe, protective horseshoes are placed in a downward-facing position, but in some parts of Ireland and Britain people believe that the shoes must be turned upward or "the luck will run out."

In 2003, I was asked to investigate a historical house in the town of Hartville, located in northern Stark County. Inside this more than one-hundred-year-old home, one could not help but notice at least fifty crosses hanging on the interior walls. In the master bedroom alone I counted fifteen. The owners were very religious, of course, and held strong faith in their Christian symbols. Upon investigating the property, it became apparent that the older couple was not only religious but superstitious as well. Various German hex signs were hung on the walls and even stenciled onto the paint in the living room. Horseshoes were hung over doorways, and bowls of salt were on shelves to help soak up evil energy. I could not help but notice the cross necklace worn by the lady of the house and her various statues of religious figures on display. The house was believed by the owners to be possessed and had been ever since the elderly couple moved there just three years earlier. Odd noises upstairs and in the basement had been heard. Shadowy forms in the upstairs hallway had been seen, but only by this couple. No visitors to the home experienced anything paranormal in any way. After a six-hour investigation and reviewing hours of audio and video, there was nothing at all paranormal captured during my visit. The owners seemed almost disappointed, and I offered to come back and investigate if more activity occurred. They confided in me that they thought perhaps someone had cursed them and this was why the house seemed to be evil at times. I never heard from them again and often wonder if the entities that they believed to be there truly were…or perhaps they moved away. This couple was of German ancestry and apparently had carried these superstitions and traditions from the old country down through their family.

Superstitions still play a very visible role in twenty-first-century living and can be seen in various locations throughout the county. Next time you are in an elevator in a high-rise or a hotel, check to see if there is a thirteenth floor. Strolling the streets in Massillon, Alliance or Canton? Look up and see if you can spot gargoyles perched on top of certain buildings for protection. Walking in a local cemetery? Check out the placement of the early Christian graves. Most are placed east to west to allow the dead to easily enter heaven when they are called home. Look around the cemetery perimeter for an iron fence. It was believed at one time that ghosts were not able to cross water or iron. The iron fence was originally put up to protect the living, not the dead!

BEYOND THE TOWPATH

A Dead Irishman for Every Mile of Canal

In 1825, a great project was begun that would open up the entire state of Ohio to transportation and trade. The Ohio frontier would be connected via a canal waterway with New York and New Orleans. The Ohio & Erie Canal helped people and products flow across America, fueling westward expansion and trade. Extending 308 miles from Lake Erie to the Ohio River, the Ohio & Erie Canal completed a water route between the East Coast and the Gulf of Mexico. It was basically the "ditch" that opened up Ohio's wilderness to trade and passenger travel. On July 4, 1825, ground was broken on the canal at Licking Summit near Newark, Ohio. The Ohio & Erie Canal took seven years to complete and was finished in 1832.

With the growth that was stimulated by the canal, Ohio's population grew from 581,295 in 1820 to 1.98 million in 1850. This made Ohio the third most populous state in the union. The canal spurred Ohio's rapid growth both agriculturally and industrially. Cities such as Akron and Cleveland grew from small towns into prosperous communities bolstered by the passengers and trade on the canal route. The canal carried freight traffic from 1827 to 1861, when freight traffic rapidly diminished due to the construction of railroads across the state of Ohio. From 1862 to 1913, the canal served as a water source to industries and towns.

On March 23, 1913, after a winter of record snowfall, storms dumped an abnormally heavy amount of rain on the state of Ohio.

The *St. Helena* canalboat freighter. *Courtesy of the Canal Fulton Heritage Society Collection.*

This caused extensive flooding of creeks, rivers and the canal. The reservoirs spilled over into the canal, destroying aqueducts, washing out banks and devastating most of the locks. In Akron, one county north of Stark, Lock 1 was dynamited to allow backed-up floodwaters to flow. At least 428 people died during the flood of 1913 in Ohio alone, and more than twenty thousand homes were totally destroyed. Property damage was extensive, as many homes that were not destroyed were seriously damaged. Factories, railroads and other structures also suffered major losses.

Today, the Ohio & Erie Canalway is a National Heritage Area. It is a scenic area with trails, scenic byways and trains. There are winding rivers and lakes and rustic wooded areas. Ohio's history almost comes to life around you as you travel the route that the early "canawlers" used to transport their goods and passengers. The trail meanders through scenic areas like the Cuyahoga Valley National Park; cities like Akron and Massillon, which were once major ports along the canal; and small towns like Canal Fulton and Peninsula, whose sizes today belie their importance in the early days of the canal and both of which owe their very existence to the canal. The canal is a beautiful part of Ohio's history, but it was also the scene of darker times and tragic accidents. Tales of unmarked graves, Indian attacks, accidental drownings and ghostly apparitions linger along the canal and its towpath.

During construction of the canal, many workers of Irish ethnicity were hired for the strenuous project. Thousands upon thousands labored to build the canals. Those literally in the trenches faced extremely arduous conditions for little pay. The workers lived on the edge of subsistence financially; physically, canal work was backbreaking, dangerous and, at certain times, fraught with the near certainty of cholera and malaria, both of which carried off sizable chunks of the workforce during virulent years. The lives of many Irish immigrants who worked in the canals seem to have been, in those immortal words, "short, brutish, and nasty." Violence and heavy drinking were rampant in the communities, and armed conflicts and labor riots were far from unheard of during these early years.

In digging the canal, mud, dirt and trees were moved by backbreaking labor, with only picks, axes and shovels as the tools of the time period. Horses and mules were also used to haul soil and fell trees, but the men bore the brunt of the physical labor. Workers were typically paid thirty cents per day, with a jigger or two of whiskey to help stave off any diseases. Unfortunately, antibiotics were not invented yet, and many hardened workers succumbed to the ravages of diseases such as cholera, dysentery and malaria. Poor living conditions helped the spread of vermin and disease, as did poor-quality drinking water. Cholera was spread through contaminated water and food, but it was not a known fact at that time. People who contracted this illness would often die from dehydration within a few hours.

The Scots-Irish seemed to suffer the most. The local legend that surrounds the canal says that for every mile of canal, a dead Irishman lies buried in its banks. The poor souls who perished could not afford proper burial in many area churchyard cemeteries, as they had no funds to pay for decent burials. Many a lone worker fell dead and was simply buried in a shallow grave dug along the steep

C.R. Dailey Furniture and Undertaker, Canal Fulton. *Courtesy of the Canal Fulton Heritage Society Collection.*

banks of the canal. It is said that in life we seek acknowledgement and in death we seek the same. If a grave is not acknowledged or marked properly, many believe that the soul does not rest as it should. Could this be what fuels the paranormal activity along the old towpath and canal? If the legend is correct, and there is at least one body for every mile of canal, then there would be at least 308 bodies in unmarked graves along the towpath trail, as the canal travels this many miles before it reaches the Ohio River.

Many local Native Americans were displeased with the canal way and the encroaching settlers. The canal business was subject to a few Indian raids and unfortunate murders. These attacks never made the front page of newspapers, as they would frighten off prospective travelers on the canal ways. Nonetheless, these dark deeds happened to some unlucky travelers and workers. There were frequent accidental drownings in the canal as well. Canalboat captains who lived on the boats had their entire families onboard with them. Occasionally one of the children would slip quietly overboard, not to be discovered until it was too late. There have been photographs taken of small children tied to wooden stakes on top of the canalboats to help them avoid falling to their watery deaths.

Other dark tales surround a specific area of the canal in Stark County. Lock 4 Park is situated one mile south of Canal Fulton on Erie Street. It is maintained by Ohio Stark Parks and is a beautiful area to picnic in or to let the kids play freely in the playground area. Glancing around at the canal and park-like setting, it is hard to imagine anything but beauty at this location. History is not always pretty, and what allegedly happened here at Lock 4 in the late nineteenth century is evidence of that.

Many canal workers and boatmen had gotten word that the railroad was blazing a trail through the area and that the canal era would be rolling to a close. Railroads could ship people and transport goods quicker than a four-mile-per-hour canalboat could ever dream of traveling. Many canawlers became outraged at the railroad companies and all they stood for. Rallies took place, and people became desperate as their way of life and incomes were threatened by the closing of the canal.

Lock 4 in Canal Fulton. *Photo by Mason Recco.*

Local legend says that one canal worker became violent and grabbed a container of some kind of caustic liquid that was being transported on a canalboat. The enraged worker tossed the lid open and flung the contents on his fellow workers, dumping the remnants on himself. Legend states that no immediate deaths ensued, but rather the men suffered gruesome, slower deaths that took several days. A few men perished due to their acid-eaten skin and organs. The man responsible also died. Some claim that if you visit Lock 4 today and listen closely, you can hear the cries and moans of the men who suffered this tragic event. No documentation has been found to this date to certify that this tragedy took place, but it has been part of local legend and lore for many years. This incident is mentioned in a book by author Jeff Belanger in 2004 called *The World's Most Haunted Places*.

Many people have confided in me over the years that they have seen shadowy figures while out strolling along certain sections of the towpath. Local newspapers from the 1960s and 1970s in Stark County spoke of this very fact, stating that "Ghostly Canal Workers Stroll Towpath." Why would these pathways and waterways be haunted? Many paranormal researchers believe that ghosts tend to linger due to a job left unfinished. Could it be that the canal workers continue their ghostly work along the canal? Is their presence due to the fact that there are numerous unmarked graves gracing the banks of the canal? Another reason that spirits may linger is due to the fact their lives were cut short by a tragic death. Surely the children who drowned falling off the boats and into the murky canal water would enter this category.

I am sure that skeptics will be able to reason away any odd feelings along the towpath that they may experience. Perhaps that sudden chill is just that and nothing more. Take a stroll along the towpath some day as the sun starts to sink in the sky. I bet you will glance over your shoulder more than once or twice.

THE UNDERGROUND RAILROAD

Tunnels, Hidden Rooms and Ghosts in Gray and Blue

Harriet Beecher Stowe was an American author and abolitionist in the years before the American Civil War. Stowe was born on June 14, 1811, in Litchfield, Connecticut. In 1832, the Beecher family moved to Cincinnati, Ohio. During the 1830s, Stowe became an abolitionist. Slavery had been prohibited north of the Ohio River since the passage of the Northwest Ordinance of 1787. Cincinnati was immediately north of the state of Kentucky, where slavery was legal. Many slaves used Ohio as their escape route to points north and to Canada as well. Harriet published the stories that she heard while living in Cincinnati in 1852 and sold more than 500,000 copies in the first five years. Her book brought slavery to life for many Northerners. It did not necessarily make these people devoted abolitionists, but the book began to move more and more Northerners to consider ending the evil institution of slavery. Those living in Stark County, for the most part, cast their lot with the Union during the American Civil War.

The Underground Railroad is a difficult topic to research, as paper trails are scarce and actual documentation is rare. The Underground Railroad was an informal network of secret routes and safe houses used by nineteenth-century black slaves in the United States to escape to free states and Canada with the aid of abolitionists who were sympathetic to their cause. The Fugitive Slave Law forced runaways to flee to Canada, Mexico, the Caribbean and even Europe.

If you were caught harboring runaway slaves in Stark County, you could be thrown in jail and charged under the Fugitive Slave

Law of 1850. This was one of the most controversial acts of the 1850 compromise and heightened Northern fears of a "slave power conspiracy." It declared that all runaway slaves be brought back to their masters and any person aiding a runaway slave by providing food or shelter was subject to six months' imprisonment and a $1,000 fine. Officers who captured a fugitive slave were entitled to a bonus for their work. Slave owners only needed to supply an affidavit to a Federal marshal to capture an escaped slave.

Stark County has twelve known sites listed as stations on the Underground Railroad. They are: the J. Ridgeway House in Alliance; the Red House in Marlboro Township; the John S. Wallace Farm in Washington Township; the Richard Elson Homestead in Magnolia; the Mount Union College area in Alliance; the Old Hartville Inn in Hartville; the Hiram Wellman House in Massillon; the Spring Hill Home in Massillon; the Rochester House in Navarre; the New Baltimore Inn in New Baltimore; the Robert Folger House in Massillon; and the Jacob Gaskin Farm in North Canton.

A most unlikely stop on the Underground Railroad is now part of a golf course and country club. Fairways of North Canton in Stark County has historical value, as its property was a known

The Pantry, the Old Hartville Inn in Hartville. *Courtesy of the Allan Conrad Collection.*

stop on the Underground Railroad. This property was once that of former slave Jacob Gaskins. Jacob was the first black man in Plain Township to vote and was an instrumental figure in helping runaway slaves seek refuge and freedom. Jacob was known locally to neighborhood children as "Black Jake." He was born in 1792 in Winchester County, Virginia. His owner freed all of his nearly one thousand slaves upon his death, with the exception of those slaves under the age of twenty-one. Jacob was one of these too young to be freed, so he went to work for another master, who admired him for his hard work and honesty. The new master freed Jacob, but he continued to work for him and shared in the profits as well.

In 1817, Jacob Gaskins gathered his earnings and came to Stark County. Jacob then started a small farm in Plain Township, which is now the Fairways of North Canton golf course. By the time the 1820 census was recorded, the Gaskins family was one of five "free colored" families living in Stark County. At that time, nearly twelve hundred people lived in the county. There were not many blacks living in the county at that time due to the fact that they had to post a $500 bond to live in the state of Ohio so that they did not become a burden on the county or state. But Jacob Gaskins persevered and gained great respect locally. When he died, Gaskins owned 375 acres of property, quite a feat for a former slave from Virginia.

One documented building used as a safe house for runaway slaves in Stark County is Spring Hill Home. Spring Hill is located in Massillon and was built in 1812. It was the home of Thomas and Charity Rotch, a Quaker couple from New England. While their home was being built, the couple lived in a log cabin on their four-thousand-acre Spring Hill Farm, where they raised merino sheep. Thomas founded the nearby town of Kendal, which has become part of Massillon. Charity started an early vocational school near their home. Thomas and Charity used their home as a safe haven for slaves escaping to freedom in the North. Charity mentioned this practice in her journal and in an 1821 letter to her sister in the East. By 1820, before the construction of the house, slaves had been harbored in the upper story of their simple log springhouse. After their new house was erected, the Rotches housed runaway slaves in the basement area and the second floor. In the new abode, a hidden staircase led directly from the basement to the second floor. Hidden rooms and passageways are common in safe houses. Often, the main home was not suited to harbor the slaves and they were instructed to stay in the root cellar, barn or springhouse.

On several occasions, I have spoken to people over the years who have visited Spring Hill on a tour. These folks did not necessarily consider themselves sensitive or psychic, but they all experienced the same type of sensations in certain areas of the house. There are two rooms that people have mentioned to me where they feel as if they are being watched or as if they have walked into something they cannot see with the naked eye. In other words, as one woman described to me, she felt as if there were a "presence" in the room. While I know of no documented haunting in the home, it's interesting to note that several people have picked up on this feeling while there on visits. Paranormal researchers all agree that energy can imprint itself on the atmosphere, and perhaps this is just a residual feeling that was left behind. Imagine the fear, desperation and loneliness felt by some of these poor slaves as they ran for their very lives. Imagine wives separated from husbands and children and the angst felt during the separation. Perhaps they would never see each other again. It is possible that these strong feelings imprinted themselves in the areas where they were experienced. Residual energy and imprinted energy are said to linger in locations where trauma, death and intense feelings occurred. Spring Hill may just be one of these places. Several original outbuildings remain on the farm, including a springhouse, wool house, smokehouse and milk house.

Another such home used on the Underground Railroad is in Alliance, located on the eastern side of Stark County. Alliance was formerly called "Crossing" because it developed at the junction of two lines on the Pennsylvania Railroad. The Haines House served as an Underground Railroad station in Alliance beginning about 1853. Its owners were Jonathan Ridgeway Haines and Sarah Grant Haines, who were Quaker farmers. They were active abolitionists in an area that Underground Railroad historian Wilbur Seibert characterized as "a hotbed of abolition." Legend states that the slaves would be protected by Mr. Haines and his gun as they hid out in an attic room. The old Haines House sat on 126 acres of land less than one hundred yards from what was one of the easternmost Underground Railroad trails in Ohio. This road is now known as State Route 183. According to Wilbur Siebert's map, Alliance sat as a focal point of Underground Railroad trails that led from three points—Mechanicstown and Hanoverton from the south and Salem from the east. Mr. Haines died in 1899 and Mrs. Haines followed in 1903. They are buried in Alliance City Cemetery, and their home is now being revitalized by the Alliance Area Preservation Society.

In Marlboro Township in Stark County, there stands a home known for its history on the Underground Railroad. It was built by Kersey G. Thomas and was erected in 1850. Thomas was of the Quaker faith. The first Quakers showed up in the seventeenth century about the same time the English translation of the Bible was printed. Quakers were first called "Seekers," and they did not agree with the Christianity of their day. Quakers believe in pacifism and that Christians should not fight with carnal weapons. Thomas followed suit and did not believe in slavery among mankind. He provided sanctuary to all runaway slaves heading north to Canada. He joined protest groups and served as an officer in the Portage County Anti-Slavery Society, acting as vice-president at one time. Kersey Thomas is listed in records found on microfilm as donating money to the antislavery movement. There are records to prove that this home was used on the Underground Railroad and it is now a verified stop along Ohio's Underground Railroad.

In the home that Kersey Thomas built, there is a secret room tucked away on the second floor, just off the small attic. No window graces this secret room, as that would give its presence away to someone outside. The room could be entered by removing a piece of the sloping ceiling panel. The ceiling beams below the hidden room give the illusion that the ceiling is of standard height. The design helps camouflage the upper room when looking at the house from the outside. The room is ten by eleven feet and can hold about ten to twelve people. This home joins nearly twelve hundred other historical sites on the Ohio Underground Railroad, and its value is great, as it stands as a reminder of human fortitude. The

Thomas house is known locally as "the Red House" and is on the direct route used by runaway slaves traveling from Canton to Hartville.

Another prominent Stark County resident who was active in the antislavery movement was Ellis N. Johnson, the founder of the village of Mount Union. Mr. Johnson was born on April 1, 1789, and died on September 15, 1889. He was the proud father of sixteen children and was very involved in the Underground Railroad movement in the county. He was a personal friend of John Brown and also served as mayor of Mount Union for two terms. He lived to be one hundred years old and was affectionately known by many as Uncle Ellis.

There are several other locations in Stark County that are rumored to have been used on the Underground Railroad, but none of them has documentation. In the quaint canal town of Canal Fulton, there are rumors that the 1870s building that houses Sisters Century House Restaurant may have been used as a station

Ellis N. Johnson, a staunch antislavery supporter. *Courtesy of the Alliance Historical Collection.*

A Ghoulish History

The old tunnel entrance in the basement of Sisters Century House Restaurant. *Photo by Sherri Brake.*

on the Underground Railroad. One only has to think of the Civil War dates to realize that this is not possible. The building that houses Sisters Century House Restaurant was built in 1870. The American Civil War ended in 1865, five years before the building was even erected. There is no way that the tunnel in the basement was used to harbor slaves.

Another location in Stark County that was rumored to have been used on the Underground Railroad is the little Pink House on North Canal Street in Canal Fulton. This house was built in 1842 and has been a private home, a gift shop and now houses a commercial business. There is what appears to be a tunnel entrance in the basement area of the building. I have personally crawled back into the area under this building, and if there was a tunnel, not much of it was left as of 2003.

There have been massive floods that have affected the area, specifically the 1913 flood, which may have caused some of these tunnels to collapse or close off. Rumors have spread locally of the possibility of slaves being harbored in the tunnel that was said to

The brick wall entrance in the basement of the Pink House, Canal Fulton. *Photo by Sherri Brake.*

Big stone blocks in an alleged tunnel area under the Pink House. *Photo by Sherri Brake.*

run under Canal Street and connect with the Ohio & Erie Canal. Once again, no documentation exists and this is merely speculation. It does, however, make a great story!

With the outbreak of the American Civil War in April 1861, the majority of Ohioans cast their lots with the Union. The state raised nearly 320,000 soldiers for the Union army, third behind only New York and Pennsylvania in total manpower contributed to the military. Ohio troops fought in nearly every major campaign during the war, with nearly 7,000 Ohio soldiers killed in action. Stark County played an active role in training soldiers. Massillon was home to a Union training camp. The 104th and 115th Ohio Volunteer Infantries were mustered in at this location.

William McKinley Jr. was the twenty-fifth president of the United States and was born in Niles, Ohio. He was the last veteran

A Pink House window. Ghostly shadows have been reported here. *Photo by Sherri Brake.*

The Pink House in Canal Fulton. *Photo by Sherri Brake.*

of the American Civil War to be elected as president. In June 1861, at the start of the Civil War, he enlisted in the Union army as a private in the Twenty-third Regiment, Ohio Volunteer Infantry. He has many ties to Stark County, and the county has honored him in many ways, the William McKinley Presidential Library and Museum being one of these. Canton was a significant location in McKinley's life, as he lived there and also practiced there as an attorney. His final resting place, McKinley Memorial Mausoleum, is one of grandeur and awe. William McKinley was also the first president to appear on film extensively. His inauguration was the first presidential inauguration to be filmed. Most of the films were recorded by the Edison Company.

President and Mrs. McKinley attended the Pan-American Exposition in Buffalo, New York, on September 5, 1901, and the president gave a public speech while in town. Leon Frank Czolgosz waited in line with a pistol in his right hand that was concealed by a handkerchief. Czolgosz fired twice at the president. McKinley's doctors believed that he would recover from the shooting, and the

President McKinley as a young Union soldier. *Courtesy of the* Canton Repository *Collection.*

president rested for more than a week in Buffalo. McKinley then began to go into shock. At 2:15 a.m. on September 14, 1901, eight days after he was shot by Czolgosz, President McKinley died from gangrene. His last words were: "It is God's way; His will be done, not ours." President McKinley's tomb and the McKinley Museum are a must-see while visiting the Canton area.

Ghost stories seem to abound when one speaks of devastation and death. The Civil War in America brought both of these facts home to many residents. This was the first time that a war had been photographed every step of the way. Matthew Brady and Alexander Gardner took photographs that made the front page of local newspapers. Death, disease and the destruction of life as it was known affected every family, whether they cast their lot with the South or the North. Hundreds of thousands of young boys and men were struck down by the hand of battle and the agony of disease and starvation. Many paranormal investigators agree that areas where battles have taken place are very active locations. To many of us, these beautiful rolling battlefields are just that—places to picnic or perhaps take scenic photos. Pausing at some of these sites and reflecting on the horrors of war is not a pleasant pastime. No such battles took place in Stark County, but many a soldier lies buried in the cemeteries that dot the county's landscape. Take a stroll through the Massillon cemetery on Erie Street and pause at the large monument to the Union soldiers buried there. Some of the graves possess names and some are simply titled "unknown." Most are under the age of twenty-five and were part of the units mustered in at Camp Massillon. (The location that Camp Massillon occupied is now the location of Oak Knoll Park in Massillon, Ohio.)

It is interesting to note that on our nighttime lantern walks through the Massillon cemetery, there have been quite a few participants who have been intrigued by some of the feelings they experienced near the monument. Those who are sensitive or tend to be psychic have sometimes picked up on a bit of sadness in this area, and it makes perfectly good sense. These were boys and men struck down in the prime of their lives. They gave their lives so that our nation could secure itself in unity. This white marble soldiers' monument at the

A Ghoulish History

Massillon cemetery is decorated beautifully every Memorial Day and was commissioned in 1871 by the Grand Army of the Republic. It is certainly the most impressive statue in the cemetery.

There have been several locations that I have investigated over the last twenty odd years in Stark County that have involved possible ghosts of the Civil War. The most notable investigation took place in the Tuslaw area of western Stark County. The farmhouse in question stood solitary in the fields that cover most of that area of the county. A beautiful rolling landscape dotted with old farms and cornfields is typical of this area of Ohio. The house was rumored to have been haunted and not only featured a human ghost or two but animal ghosts as well. This home was said to have been built over a site of tragedy. Violent deaths had occurred here in an arson fire back in the early 1800s. The farmhouse was built over the remains of an old trading post, where a husband, wife and all of their children perished. Odd noises, apparitions and smells have plagued this property through several tenants. During a time when the house was vacant, witchcraft symbols were said to have been painted by trespassers.

One of the ghosts in question at this location in Tuslaw is that of Robert Green, who was said to have been a Union soldier in the Civil War. Legend states that Robert paid his way into a high rank and served his country faithfully. Mr. Green was said to have sustained wounds to one of his legs, which required amputation. It is his one-legged and wooden-stumped image that people have both seen and heard at this location. Occupants of this home have shared with me the fact that they researched this property diligently throughout the years that they occupied the premises. Mr. Green was said to have fallen in the barn from a ladder and died on location from injuries to his neck. His ghost has been seen by several people, and he has allegedly conversed with a small boy who lived here in the 1970s. Why would a ghost hang out at any location? Paranormal theories suggest that people who haunt their properties do so because of a sense of duty, pride in their home or just plain stubbornness. Perhaps Mr. Green loved his land and home to the extent that he wants to guard over it in the afterlife.

The American Civil War claimed nearly 600,000 soldiers, according to many sources. The numbers are varied depending on which source is quoted, but the bottom line is the fact that this was the deadliest and bloodiest war in the history of our nation. No one was spared and everyone was affected, whether they tried to remain impartial or cast their lots with the North or South. The Civil War touched everyone in Stark County. Venture into almost any cemetery in the county and the evidence is written on many of the stones found there. Ghosts are said to abound in areas of trauma, tragedy and unfinished business, and each death that occurred during the Civil War certainly meets those requirements. It is no wonder that so many who wander the old cemeteries and battlefields today are affected by feelings of sadness. It was Ohio's own General William Tecumseh Sherman who said:

> *You don't know the horrible aspects of war. I've been through two wars and I know. I've seen cities and homes in ashes. I've seen thousands of men lying on the ground, their dead faces looking up at the skies. I tell you, war is hell!*

BURY THE DEAD

Digging Up Local Cemetery Legends

Because I could not stop for Death,
He kindly stopped for me.
The Carriage held but just ourselves
And Immortality.
—Emily Dickinson

Our death is not an end if we can live on in our children and the younger
generation. For they are us, our bodies are only wilted leaves on the tree of life.
—Albert Einstein

One can be certain that in any county in the state of Ohio, there are certain local legends that persist over the decades. There are legends that surround various cry baby bridges, old vacant buildings, spooky hollows, remote railroad tracks, abandoned asylums and hospitals and creepy backwoods areas. Many of these legends are just that—legend. No basis can be found in actual fact or documentation, and the stories lend themselves to the category of urban legend. Cemetery legends are not a scarcity across the Buckeye State. There are ghosts that are said to visit certain graves on the anniversary of their deaths. There have been reports of mysterious balls of glowing light and unusual smells of cigars and women's perfume in remote cemeteries when no one is around. There have been graves on which flowers mysteriously appear. There are cemeteries where ladies in gray and ladies in

One Way sign, Massillon cemetery. *Photo by Dianne Blosser.*

white have been spotted. Other legends develop as visitors swear they hear voices screaming inside a cemetery late at night, or perhaps they claim to see an ethereal image walking among the graves. Various reports of hounds of hell and ghost dogs find their place in cemetery folklore across the state. There have been reports of glowing headstones, large marble balls that rotate mysteriously on their perches and mausoleum doors that swing open and shut as if of their own accord.

The mystique of a cemetery appeals to some people and frankly scares most others away. Many of us enjoy walking through cemeteries, photographing various monuments, doing grave rubbings (not recommended) and reading the epitaphs of old. There is a name given to this eclectic bunch: we are called taphophiles. A taphophile is someone who has a passion for and enjoyment of cemeteries. We are all sisters and brothers in the hands of mortality and our preoccupation. The opposite of a taphophile would be someone who suffers from placophobia, or a fear of cemetery tombstones. Those who suffer from placophobia may find themselves sweating and shaking when visiting a cemetery.

Their hearts may race and they might find it difficult to breathe. They might find themselves inventing excuses to avoid visiting cemeteries altogether.

The fascination and fear surrounding death has been around since the start of time. Death is the great equalizer. No matter your religion, income, gender or ethnicity, death comes to us all in the end. The Victorian era was brought into being by England's Queen Victoria. Queen Victoria had made mourning a fashionable tradition. Her husband, Prince Albert, died of typhoid in 1861. She dressed her entire court in mourning attire and remained in full mourning clothes for three years. A death during Victorian times required long periods of mourning traditions and was accompanied by many grief rituals. The longest mourning period was for the death of a spouse and usually lasted a minimum of two years. Many widows spent the rest of their lives in full mourning attire, donning a black veil and gloves to complement their black dress.

"Show me your cemeteries and I will show you what kind of people you have," said Benjamin Franklin. This statement continues

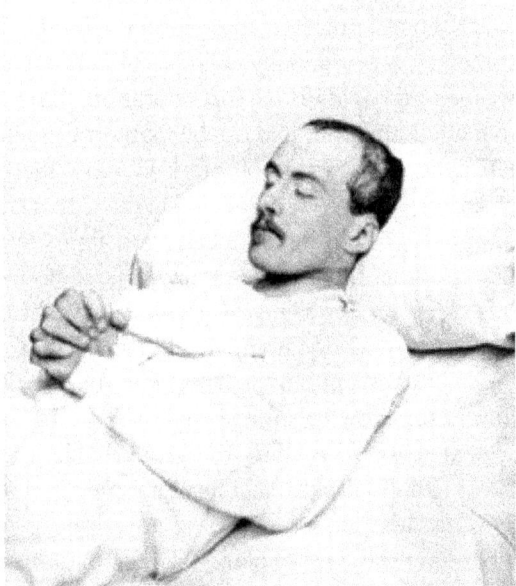

A typical death image during the Victorian era. *Courtesy of the Sherri Brake Collection.*

to ring true today. We can tell so much from the artwork, style and type of monuments erected. Each stone tells a story, and each cemetery has its own tale. Cemeteries can tell us much about our ancestors, their occupations, their social status and their beliefs. Information can be gleaned from the words carved on stones. We can learn a great deal concerning family relationships from the placement of a grave within the cemetery. The cemetery itself becomes a repository of expression, human values and beliefs.

In Stark County, there are several cemeteries that harbor legends, ghostly lore and interesting characters. In West Lawn Cemetery in Canton, there is a headstone that simply has the name "Frankenstein" engraved on its smooth granite face. There are numerous websites and stories circulated of paranormal activity that happens near this grave. Once again, the hype is steeped in urban legend and the fascination that surrounds the name of Frankenstein. West Lawn Cemetery is also the final resting place for many of Canton's founders and elite society. The Harters, the Hoovers, the McKinleys, the Danners, the Aultmans, the Beldens, the Gibbs and the Saxtons are all recognized names locally and have left their marks on this area's history. The first burial in West Lawn Cemetery took place on January 1, 1861. Ada B. Wright, age two, was interred after losing a battle with diphtheria. This cemetery was originally called the Canton Cemetery, but its name was changed after its incorporation. The cemetery is owned, managed and operated by the Canton Cemetery Association.

In the eastern side of Stark County, there is allegedly a small shack on the grounds of a Jewish cemetery in Alliance that is haunted by blue lights. These odd lights show up at night from time to time. Blue and white lights have been reported in and near this cemetery for many years. Balls of light or glowing orbs have been seen and documented. These balls of light can look like a huge luminescent bubble floating in the air. They usually appear as mysterious glowing spheres that drift through the air. They can also appear to bounce along the ground. Light balls are described as glowing balls of plasma. The phenomena usually last for only about five seconds but sometimes remain longer, up to a few minutes. There are different explanations for these balls of light. Some are

A Ghoulish History

The Frankenstein grave, West Lawn Cemetery. *Photo by Sherri Brake.*

scientific and some border on the paranormal. Ball lightning has also been seen without any detected electrical storm. Some people believe that ball lightning movement is guided by electromagnetic fields, or EM energies. The pioneers feared these balls of light and believed them to be a precursor to a traumatic event.

In Canal Fulton, and located on a hill west of the Tuscarawas River, there lies a small cemetery forgotten by many. The Pioneer Cemetery sits behind the Methodist church and was there many years before the church was built. Many of the founding pioneers and their children lie buried in this quaint cemetery. These stones stand as a testament to the trials of the frontier and its immigrants. The majority of the stones are difficult to read, and some are carved in German. Many Germans were buried here and their names are almost lost to time. A cemetery listing shows fewer than thirty names, but there are twice that many interred here. One such grave is that of little Madison. This little boy died from drowning in June 1816. There have been odd occurrences near his grave, and many people who have visited claim to have recorded EVP, or electronic voice phenomena, on tape recording devices. I have heard some of these tapes and it truly does sound like children speaking. Electronic voice phenomena piqued the interest of Thomas Edison, who was said to be working on a spirit communicator before his death in 1931.

Another grave of interest in this little pioneer cemetery is that of John Edgington. John was a soldier in the Revolutionary War, enlisted in Captain James Munn's battalion in Washington County, Pennsylvania. He survived the war against England and moved to Stark County, where he lived until his death. No marker stands to honor this soldier, but an Ohio bicentennial marker was erected in his honor. I contacted the Daughters of the American Revolution in 2003, and we held a ceremony to honor this man and his efforts as a Patriot. Information is scarce for this gentleman, and it is hoped that future researchers may be able to compile the pieces of the puzzle.

While on the subject of forgotten graves and soldiers of the past, I can think of several others who deserve recognition. J. Adam Fisher was born in 1763 and is buried in St. Jacobs Lutheran Church cemetery in Jackson Township. He died in 1841 and is buried next to his wife, Susanna. He served with Captain Krauss's company of the Third Battalion in the Buck County, Pennsylvania militia.

George Harsh was born in 1759 and died in 1833. He lies buried next to his wife, Catherine, in the Newman Baptist Church in Lawrence Township. He served in the Revolutionary War with Captain Miars's company of rangers out of Washington County, Pennsylvania.

Adam Koch was born in Germany in 1756 and died in 1844. He was a Revolutionary War solider and lies buried next to his wife, Barbara, in the Old Lutheran Cemetery on Fourth Street in Navarre. He served with Captain Craig's regulars at Yorktown, and his grave has been honored by the local Daughters of the American Revolution chapter.

One cemetery that holds a story of interest in Stark County is Niesz Cemetery. This is a small burying ground located in Canton Township at the Perry Township border. John Niesz is buried here. As a young man, he was without religion and was said to be a sinful man. He allegedly was part of a group of people that published a paper in favor of marriage infidelity, an act that would have been quite scandalous in the 1800s. Mr. Niesz passed away in 1831 and was said to have found religion due to one of his children passing at a young age. The child in question passed away in front of his father while shouting praises to the Lord. His father was affected greatly by this event.

Captain Mayhew Folger. *Courtesy of the Massillon Museum Collection.*

Mr. Niesz became a man of the cloth and was ordained as a minister in 1841.

Can you imagine the grave of a seafaring captain situated in the middle of Ohio? That is an odd enough occurrence, but imagine this grave being emptied by possible grave robbers. Sound even more intriguing? Such it is with the grave of Captain Mayhew Folger. The good captain's white headstone is located in the Massillon cemetery on South Erie Street. It has been said for many years that a man retiring from an occupation at sea will go as far inland as he can so as not to succumb to the lure of the ocean sounds. This could be the case of Captain Folger. Mayhew was a ship's captain and whaler aboard the *Topaz*, and he rediscovered the Pitcairn Islands in 1808. Have you seen the movie or read the book *Mutiny on the Bounty*? Captain Folger rescued some of the survivors of that famed ship when he found Pitcairn Island. He was a respected man in his community and became the first postmaster of Massillon when the post office was created there in 1828. He also operated an inn at the northeast corner of Main and Erie Streets. Mayhew Folger was born on March 9, 1774, and died on September 1, 1898. He was a first cousin three times removed of Benjamin Franklin. He was originally buried in the Union Cemetery in Massillon. Upon an order that his grave be moved, he was unearthed and was shockingly discovered to not possess space in his coffin. In other words, the grave had been robbed and the captain's body was missing. We have led thousands of visitors on our nighttime lantern walks through the Massillon cemetery, and the captain's grave is always one of interest to many visitors. Perhaps it is because his

Sherri Brake at Captain Mayhew's grave marker with orb. *Photo by Marcy Miller.*

story is so unusual, or maybe it's the fact that his grave is empty. Or could it be that unusual balls of light have been photographed both in the day and at night near his marker?

Massillon cemetery is maintained by the Massillon Cemetery Association, which was organized in 1846. It is one of the most interesting cemeteries I have ever had the privilege of visiting. It is historic, well maintained and truly a wonderful place to explore.

Union Cemetery in Massillon was a cemetery like many others in Ohio that sprung up from the epidemic cholera. The cholera epidemics in Ohio ravaged the population during several outbreaks in the 1800s. People who contract cholera generally suffer from severe diarrhea, vomiting and cramps. The disease is spread by drinking water or eating food that is contaminated with human feces and can cause death within a day or so after contact. Canals provided a relatively stagnant source of water that allowed cholera to fester. As a result of the stagnant water, canal workers commonly died from this deadly illness.

Cholera ran rampant in the 1830s, and it was at this time that Massillon's Union Cemetery came into existence. There are reports of mass graves at this location due to the quick deaths ensuing from the cholera outbreak. Most mass graves in this area were said to be dug to a depth of nine feet. In 1867, city workers unearthed many bones at the Union Cemetery and were puzzled, as this cemetery was to have been moved years before. Many homes were being built in the area and were placed on old graves unknowingly. To this very day, residents in the area find fragments of human bones while digging for pools or ponds or while renovating their homes by adding additions. Ghostly apparitions, water running down doors and unusual smells and sounds, as well as rocking chairs rocking themselves, have plagued many homeowners in this subdivision. Numerous paranormal investigations have occurred in several of the homes in this area. Not a year goes by that I am not contacted by a homeowner or visitor inquiring about this area and its haunted history. This area of Massillon certainly brings to mind the Hollywood movie *Poltergeist*.

In most instances, cemeteries are planned in advance and organized carefully. Occasionally, small cemeteries arise out of

The Hall Building, Massillon State Psychiatric Hospital, 1898. *Courtesy of the Karen Kline Collection.*

immediate need and are basically forgotten about if not marked properly for one reason or another. Such is the case with the unmarked graves dotting the rolling landscape of the old Massillon State Psychiatric Hospital. Massillon State Hospital for the Insane opened in 1898. Various past employees of the old hospital have told of graves dug for small children who died at birth and were sired by hospital patients. The patients were deemed indigent by the state and had no next of kin. Patients with mental illnesses would occasionally become pregnant and, with the lack of medical care or due to the physical abnormalities of the child, would miscarry the baby. Impromptu graves were allegedly dug and bodies were quietly laid to rest. In 2004, I interviewed a city worker who had run a small piece of earth-moving equipment on the site, digging for the local golf course. The golf course adjoined the old Massillon State Hospital property and was once part of the original hospital grounds. He informed me that they did indeed find bones at several times and once had found a small box while digging on a project. The worker stated that they were very anxious about the find and had imagined that it contained a small human body, but when they opened the box it contained the carcass of a dog—much to their relief!

Heading a bit south of Massillon brings you to the quaint community of Navarre, which was founded in 1806. A missionary,

A Ghoulish History

Christian Frederick Post, built the first dwelling, a log cabin, in southeastern Bethlehem Township in 1761. The 1830s brought the Ohio & Erie Canal, which opened up this area to trade and passenger travel. Navarre was the home of Orlando Poe, a United States Army officer in the American Civil War. Poe was an engineer and was basically responsible for much of the early lighthouse construction on the Great Lakes.

In Navarre, there are several beautiful, well-maintained cemeteries. One of these cemeteries has a rather interesting story. Dr. Nathan E. Coffin died in 1828. There have been several reports of the scent of cigar smoke in the area of Dr. Coffin's grave that cannot be explained. Unexplained smells in cemeteries can catch you off guard and leave you wondering about their origin. Paranormal researchers call this an olfactory manifestation. Many times these events of unexplained scents will occur just prior to or just after a visual or auditory apparition. Other common scents can include women's perfume (usually rose, lavender or lilac), baking bread, gun smoke, alcohol and pipe or cigar smoke. I have found that in most cases the smells can be directly associated with the person responsible for the activity or haunting of the area.

There are many small cemeteries that dot the rolling landscape of Stark County. One such cemetery is Sixteen Reformed Cemetery on Route 93, south of Massillon in Tuscarawas Township. In this small church cemetery, you will find a large rugged boulder denoting the burial location of Adam Poe. In the census, he is listed as a farmer, frontiersman, shoemaker and Indian fighter. Adam Poe and his brother, Andrew, were local pioneer settlers who, in 1782, led a group of men to fight the Wyandots along the Ohio River. This bloody battle took place on Yellow Creek along the Ohio River Valley and resulted in a violent fight to the death for many of the participants.

During the summer of 1782, a party of Wyandot Indians traveled through what is now the state of West Virginia and killed an old man warming himself by his cabin fire. The marauding Indians took what treasures they could find, such a food, money and various household items. Word of this viscous deed spread around the area, causing fear and concern among the pioneers. A frontier party of eight settlers struck out to find the Indians. Two of the men were Adam and Andrew Poe. These brothers were about the same size and build, standing at six feet tall and 190 pounds each. It was not an easy task to trail the Indian party through the underbrush, but the Poe brothers were steadfast and earnest in their efforts to seek out the murderers. Traveling around the west fork of the Little Beaver River and nearing Yellow Creek, they stumbled upon the Indians in question. Andrew came upon the large Indian chief, who was startled by the ambush. Andrew drew up his gun to fire, but the rifle failed to discharge. Andrew dropped his misfired gun and sprang into action, overtaking the large Indian in hand-to-hand battle. Meanwhile, Andrew's brother Adam joined the fight in earnest. Adam and Andrew took the fight into the river amongst the Indians, guns, tomahawks and knives, and the river ran blood red with the wounds of many men. While the Poe brothers were in the heat of battle, the other settlers in their party joined in the foray. One of the settlers accidentally shot Andrew through the shoulder during the chaotic commotion of battle. Andrew survived the friendly fire and later recovered from the wound. After taking Andrew back home to heal, a frontier doctor took a silk handkerchief and drew it through the bullet wound to "cleanse" it so that no clots would form and it would drain and heal naturally. At the end of the battle, four Wyandots and their great Chief Bigfoot lay spent on the banks, with their blood spewing into the waters of Yellow Creek. This fight is known as one of the bloodiest battles on Ohio soil and caused much mourning among the Wyandot tribe. Eight of the fourteen men involved in the ambush departed this life on that hot summer day in 1782.

Adam Poe and his wife, Elizabeth, are buried in the small cemetery at Sixteen Reformed Church near Massillon. Adam's large gravestone boulder stands the test of time and probably very few who visit this cemetery realize the greatness of this frontier man. The fortitude with which he and his brother Andrew fought on that hot day in 1782 are part of this county's obscure history. On a side note, Adam and Andrew's great-grandfather was Orlando Poe, a Navarre native and Civil War soldier. Local Canton resident Julie Binegar traces her ancestry to this noted frontier family and has shared with me the fact that author Edgar Allan Poe also graces this legendary family tree.

Alliance Cemetery in Alliance holds forty-one grave sites of unknown people. There are some graves in this cemetery with majestic monuments and others that are not marked and lie barren of decoration. Section S is in the rear of the cemetery and bears simple stones and barren ground. This is Potter's Field. Most cemeteries have a section such as this, where transients and indigents are buried at no cost. Their relatives, if any, may have never known how or when they died, or that they were even buried here. The lives of forty-one souls are a mystery here in Section S. There are men, women and children buried here. Some died of natural causes, in accidents and also through murder. There is only one actual headstone in the unknown section. Flowers show up mysterouislely on this grave of a baby. This baby boy departed life on May 2, 1916. All that was known of this African American baby boy is the fact that he was found dead at the Pennsylvania Railroad depot in Alliance. Two women discovered his little body wrapped in newspapers in the ladies' room on that evening in May. It appeared that he had been bathed and even dusted with baby powder. His umbilical cord had not been tied, which probably caused his untimely death as he bled to death.

Another horrific death of an infant is that of a one-week-old baby found in a water well near Jennings Road in Lexington Township. This gruesome murder defies logic—the infant's head and legs were cut off and the remains placed in a plastic bag filled with lime. Lime is presumed to speed up decomposition of a body.

The Alliance Cemetery has a few other tales that can only be found through extensive research of cemetery records. One such tale is that of an Italian man of about thirty who lay in the local hospital for days after an accident. This man was discovered lying along the Fort Wayne tracks in May 1926 and was paralyzed by his wounds. He tried to speak for days but was not able to communicate. He died before he could utter his name or give any other information.

Another sad tale at the Alliance Cemetery is that of a baby found in a local creek in 1920. Still another child was found along

Glamorgan Street in 1919 and lies at rest in the cemetery. The list goes on and on and includes a John Doe in his forties who was struck and killed by a local train and a man who died from "crushing injuries" in 1911. This man died from bleeding to death and his name is unknown, just like all of the others in Potter's Field, Section S of the Alliance Cemetery. Much work went into compiling the list, which was a project of the Alliance Genealogical Society and was published in 1999. The book took three years to prepare and contains more than twenty thousand burials. It was an enormous project and is greatly appreciated by researchers.

Cemeteries in Stark County tell many stories. Take some time to venture into a few and stroll around. Many of the stones were placed here before we arrived and there will continue to be new ones placed long after we have departed. Even in this age of spiritual awakening, human beings need to come to grips with their own mortality. Hopefully we can fit ourselves into the scheme of existence and find some answers before we "buy the farm," as they say.

Much appreciation is given to the various churches, volunteers and cemetery associations that take the time to clean and maintain these silent cities of the dead.

HANG 'EM HIGH

Lynchings, Murders and Crimes of Passion

Lynching was a form of punishment for presumed criminal offenses and was often performed by self-appointed commissions, mobs or vigilantes. This often occurred without due process of law and took place in the United States before the American Civil War and afterward, from southern states to western frontier settlements. No one was completely safe from this action, and ethnic groups were the primary ones to suffer. The term *Lynch's Law* apparently originated during the American Revolution, when Charles Lynch, a Virginia justice of the peace, ordered punishment for Tory acts of loyalty. Charles Lynch was said to head up an irregular court in Virginia and was responsible for many "informal" hangings.

Lynchings in Stark County were few, but they did happen on occasion. In the state of Ohio, lynching reached a peak in 1892. In that year alone, 226 persons (155 African Americans) met death at the hands of lynch mobs, an average of over four persons per week. Ohio took action against this vigilante style of justice and enacted the Ohio Anti-Lynching Law in 1896. In 1894, Present William McKinley used the state's National Guard to put down a series of lynchings in area counties where coal miners were striking.

In olden times, butchering animals was a household chore, and putting down dangerous animals was a practical necessity of life. When the dangerous animal turned out to be man, the logic was unchanged—an eye for an eye. Poor societies could not afford to maintain unproductive members in prison, and execution provided a common-sense solution. Dating back thousands of years, hanging was practiced in Norse times, and one of Odin's nicknames was the "Gallows God." Usually, hanging was reserved as a punishment for theft. The technique of hanging changed very little over the years: both victim and executioner climbed a ladder placed against the gibbet, the noose was put around the condemned man's neck and he was pushed from the ladder. The skill of the hangman was in estimating his victim's weight and combining it with the right amount of slack rope. Too short a drop led to slow strangulation and too long a rope changed the hanging into an accidental decapitation.

The most notable lynching was that of a man who used the alias Jeff Davis. Jeff Davis was one of the many aliases adopted by a Swiss emigrant named Miller, who came to Stark County with his parents several years before the Civil War began in 1861. He was a muscular man who weighed nearly two hundred pounds. Jeff Davis spent most of his time moving in and out of jail, most notably the Ohio Penitentiary in Columbus. In the 1850s and '60s, he served time for grand larceny and was sentenced again for assault with intent to commit rape on a woman just across the Tuscarawas County border, south of Stark County. In 1873, Davis was arrested in nearby Wayne County on a minor offense and was sent to jail once more. He managed to attack the sheriff, and Davis slipped out of the cell and locked the door behind him. He then made his escape, while the sheriff was locked in the cell. It was said that it took three blacksmiths several hours before they were able to free the sheriff from the confines of his own cell, but it was too late to capture Davis. He had slipped over the county line once more and attempted to rape an eight-year-old girl. A large, angry mob of a crowd gathered to witness Davis's hearing after he was captured in Ragersville, located in Tuscarawas County. Davis insulted one of the ladies in the crowd and was hit over the head with a poker. The lights were said to go out in the town hall and that's when all hell broke loose. Davis was dragged out by his feet and pulled down the street to the edge of town. Jeff Davis was shot by various people, including three shots to his head. None of these shots killed him, but he was heard pleading for his life. Davis was unceremoniously

A Ghoulish History

An old wooden jailhouse typical of the era, Canal Fulton. *Courtesy of the Canal Fulton Heritage Society Collection.*

dragged to the intersection of Crooked Run and Ragersville Roads. A long rope was thrown over a tree, and Davis was hanged by the angry crowd. His body was cut down much later and was buried in some woods near Sugar Creek. A local doctor took it upon himself to exhume the body and hide it in his attic. Later, the local law had him rebury the body. The story of Jeff Davis and his lynching does not end there. Dr. Herman Peters ended up with Davis's skeleton and, later, Peters's son bartered the bones for a box of cigars. History can sometimes be more fascinating than fiction!

The hanging of Christian Bechtel is one of downtown Canton's darkest moments, as well as the first public execution. Mr. Bechtel was a German emigrant who had come home in the early months of 1833 drunk. He beat his wife to death while she slept in their home. After an attempt to escape the long arm of the law, he finally gave himself up and surrendered. The criminal was convicted of murder and taken to the old jail, built in 1830, located at Cleveland Avenue and Ninth Street. The old jail was two stories tall with the typical barred windows one would expect. Sheriff George Webb took care of the prisoner's needs until the execution, and he was also in charge of the execution procedure. The prisoner was made to sit on his own coffin in the back of a wagon and wore a death shroud on his head. The crowd was said to scream out for justice, and people threw various items at the criminal as he sat hooded and waiting for death.

The execution of Bechtel took place on a cold and bleak Friday morning, November 22, 1833, in downtown Canton. Reverend

Peter Herbruck of the First Reformed Church in Canton was the attending minister and was in charge of the last rites. According to the *History of the First Reformed Church of Canton*, under a deep sense of duty toward the wretched man, Reverend Herbruck said:

> *I often visited him in prison, and admonished him to repentance and conversion, and also prayed with him. His sin was a heavy burden upon his heart, and he fervently besought the Lord for pardon. According to his own testimony, he also received mercy and forgiveness.*

The confession closed with the following words:

> *Standing as I do on the confines of two worlds, I would fain raise my voice in the language of warning and exhortation, to all who may hear the tale of my guilt and its consequences. Let them shun the rock on which I split, avoid the intoxicating cup as you would the enemy of your souls. To that I can safely trace my present condition.*

The condemned man begged all in attendance to pray for him again. After the prayer, he also began to pray. His prayer was so earnest and fervent that the bystanders were moved to tears. At eleven o'clock that morning, the condemned man was led out to his execution on the scaffold. The gallows had been erected just east of Walnut Street, between Fourth and Sixth Streets, Northeast. A crowd estimated to have numbered at least twenty thousand, coming from far and near, had assembled in the commons area at the intersection of the streets. After an English sermon had been preached, there were last rites preached in German and the event was closed with prayer. According to the notes of Reverend Herbruck, the criminal's last words were: "May the blood of Jesus Christ the son of God cleanse me from all sin."

Another hanging that took place in Stark County occurred in 1873. August Pfiffer, father of five children, had experienced some marital problems. His wife was allegedly smitten with her husband's brother, Valentine. August hanged himself in the barn of the American House Hotel, which used to stand at the corner of Canal and Cherry Streets in Canal Fulton. He is buried at St. John Cemetery in Canton, and his is one of the sad cases of a love triangle gone wrong.

Three years before President William McKinley's assassination, his wife's brother, George D. Saxton, was the victim in a murder case that has become known as the "Canton tragedy." This was an event that rocked the socialite society of Canton's rich and elite. George Dewalt Saxton was born on Halloween in 1850, the only son of one of Canton's leading families. His father, James, was a banker and founder of the Canton Repository, and Ida, one of George's two sisters, was married to President William McKinley. George Saxton was a man who lived a bit on the wild side. He loved the pursuit of women, both married and single, and also enjoyed racing fast horses and bicycling.

It was about 6:00 p.m. on October 7, 1898, when the Canton police station received a telephone call reporting the murder of George Saxton. Mr. Saxton had been shot dead on the sidewalk outside the residence of a woman named Eva Althouse, a widow of doubtful reputation, at 319 Lincoln Avenue in Canton. Mr. Saxton had been called a "ladies' man" and had allegedly led several of the area's single women astray. On the night that the body was discovered, Mr. Saxton's face "was upturned, his right arm was lying over his face as if to guard it from assault and his left arm was under his body." According to the trial manuscripts, there were three bullets found in his body. The cause of death was a bullet that had shot its fiery path through his abdomen. A multitude of law enforcement officials responded to the call, and several witnesses reported seeing a woman dressed in black at the scene. The police interviewed the witnesses and then proceeded at once to arrest Annie E. George, a jilted mistress who had made many public threats against Saxton's life due to the fact that he had led her on in public and had sullied her good family name. Annie George, born Annie Ehrhart in Hanoverton, Ohio, in 1858, married a carpenter named Sample C. George. She was twenty years old when she married, and in 1883, the Georges moved with their two sons to Canton. Annie soon had the misfortune of attracting Saxton's admiring gaze.

Downtown Canton, 1930. *Courtesy of Don Myers.*

Mrs. Annie George, a married woman and mother of two, stood trial for the murder of George Saxton. In defense of Annie George, her lawyers, John C. Welty and James Sterling, flatly denied that she had committed the murder of George Saxton and also offered an alibi. After deliberating overnight, the jury acquitted Mrs. George. When the verdict was announced, hundreds of courtroom spectators roared their approval, in defiance of the court's order. Annie, surrounded by her friends and family, stood in the courtroom for a full ten minutes receiving congratulations. As strange as it seems, telegrams offering stage appearances poured in from theatrical managers and the president of the Women's Rights Club of Pittsburgh offered her $500 for one week's engagement to talk on women's rights.

Love triangles can resolve themselves, or they can end up taking a wrong turn. Such is the case of George Eckfield in 1902. His story made local news on several occasions. He had eloped with a married woman the year before and was brought to trial on charges of theft. George was smitten with Joseph Walzer's wife in Canal Fulton. Mr. Walzer ran the Empire House downtown. George

A Ghoulish History

Eckfield's love for Mrs. Walzer seemed to border a bit on obsession, according to old *Canton Repository* articles. Eckfield was employed as a night telegraph operator at the B&O Railroad station in Canal Fulton and was a resident of nearby Massillon. In late November 1902, Eckfield had a liveryman from Massillon drive him to Canal Fulton, where he set out with a plan. Along the route, Eckfield had the liveryman stop at several establishments to drink liquor. At the last stop, he brandished a .38-caliber pistol and informed the driver that he was going to Fulton to cause three funerals. His plan was to kill Canal Fulton mayor McCadden and Joseph Walzer and then turn the gun on himself.

After arriving in Canal Fulton, Eckfield first went to the Empire House. People inside the establishment saw the drunken man advance and locked the doors to the building. Eckfield was enraged and tried to gain entry to the George Ruehling saloon. He became disorderly at the saloon and was escorted out. At this point, George Eckfield went to his place of employment, the B&O station, and used the .38-caliber pistol to end his own life. One shot through the heart ended the love triangle forever, and Eckfield lay on the station house floor bleeding to death. There were no witnesses to the deadly deed, but Station Agent Phillips was in an adjoining room at the time of the suicide. It is known among paranormal investigators that tragic events such as a suicide can sometimes leave unresolved issues on site. In other words, when someone takes his own life, there can sometimes be paranormal activity at the site where it happened. Many religions believe that taking your own life sets you up for an eternity of unresolved issues and unrest. Today, next to the train tracks in Canal Fulton, the B&O station house no longer stands. It is gone, like so much of the dark history that one can only find buried in old musty newspapers or on long rolls of microfilm archives at the local library.

Don Mellet was one of a few men who lost his life during the Prohibition era. He was gunned down near his home in Canton. Canton had earned the nickname "Little Chicago" due to the organized crime that ran rampant. On July 26, 1926, Mellet was shot, execution style, in the back of his head. Mellet was an editor at the *Canton Daily News* and had been ready to run an exclusive

Don Mellett was murdered execution style in 1926. *Courtesy of the* Canton Repository *Collection.*

article exposing the names of local men involved in crime. The article was to appear in the paper the day after his murder.

Murders and murderers have plagued society since Cain killed his brother Abel, as documented in the Christian Bible. One prior resident of Canton who was murdered was Thomas Lee Dillion. Thomas Lee Dillon was born in Canton on July 9, 1950. Dillon was a serial sniper who shot and killed five people in southeastern Ohio, beginning on April 1, 1989, and continuing until April 1992. He has been called "Ohio's Unsportsmanlike Sniper" by some and a sadist by others. A mild-mannered draftsman for a municipal water department, Thomas Dillon liked to cruise the back roads of southeastern Ohio. Like so many other serial killers, he began acting out against animals at a very young age. As a teenager, he began keeping track of all of the animals he killed on a calendar in his home on Thirty-seventh Street, Northwest. As a young teen, he started setting fires to appease his need for adventure. He would later admit to setting more than one hundred fires and killing more than one thousand pets and farm animals. His trips through the backwoods of Ohio were always taken alone, and he would stop on his way to buy beer as he cruised along looking for his next innocent victim. After high school, Dillon attended Kent State's Stark campus and then college in Columbus before returning back to Stark County. His killing rampages continued. Once, as an adult, Dillon shot a chipmunk in his backyard and then grabbed the dead animal and chased his son around the yard. When the little boy tripped and fell down on his knees, Dillon rubbed his face with the bloody carcass. Later on, Dillon was convicted of five known murders committed between the years 1989 and 1992. He is currently serving five terms of thirty years to life for aggravated murder and fifteen additional years for gun specification.

Traveling back in time a few years, we have another interesting incident in Canton's past. In the 1880 presidential election, James Garfield defeated Winfield S. Hancock, the journal *Science* was founded by Thomas Edison and the first electric streetlight was installed in Wabash, Indiana. In downtown Canton, a large wooden scaffold was being erected. It was a Friday afternoon in June in the county seat of Stark, and the town was preparing to execute three young souls in public. One of the criminals to be executed was Gustave A. Ohr. He was born in Bavaria, Germany, and had come to this country when he was just one year old. His father died, and his mother remarried, moved to Chicago and raised her son the best that she could. Ohr was said to be very musically gifted and could play the violin and other instruments. He loved to read and was sought to play music at concerts and balls. When Gustave turned seventeen, he decided to travel from his home of Chicago and moved eastward. When he neared Fort Wayne, he fell into company with two other wayward souls. One was an older man and the other a young man. The three traveled east until they came to Stark County in 1880. It was here in Stark County that the two youths murdered the old man, whose name was John Wattmaugh, while he was asleep and stole his pocket watch. Ohr was arrested and incarcerated. He was found guilty of the crime of murder and was sentenced to be hanged on June 25, 1880. The other guilty party was George E. Mann. Mann was born in New York and was of English ancestry. His mother died when he was a young child and his father remarried and moved west to Kansas. At the young age of fifteen, George took to the life of tramping or "hoboing."

One other wayward soul was executed on that hot day in June 1880. John Sammett, age seventeen, murdered a young acquaintance and was charged with burglary as well. He was of German ancestry, like Ohr, and his parents were well-respected citizens. After his mother died, John became restless and began to seek out adventure. Early in life he exhibited a fondness for excitement and satisfied these urges with petty thefts. These three boys were executed on a scaffold that had been erected in front of the Stark County Courthouse. Attendance was high that day in June and the crowd was satisfied that justice had once again been served.

Another criminal to meet his death by climbing thirteen steps to the hangman's scaffolding was George McMillian. George was executed by hanging in Canton in the year 1883 on Friday, July 20. He was convicted to the gallows for a murder he had committed earlier in the year. Another doer of evil was a man by the name of Henry Popp. Henry was thirty-one years old and was also sentenced to hang in front of a crowd of the curious minded. Popp was a railroad worker convicted of murder and was hanged by the neck until dead on December 19, 1890. Local Canton saloon owner Morris Callahan was murdered by Popp on April 21, 1890.

Since 1885, a total of 371 individuals have been executed in the state of Ohio. In 1885, the legislature enacted a law that required executions to be carried out at the Ohio Penitentiary in Columbus by hanging. In 1897, the gallows were replaced by the electric chair, which was considered to be a more technologically advanced and humane form of execution. Ohio also became the second state to use the electric chair for executions. Twenty-eight hangings and 315 electrocutions were carried out at the now defunct Ohio Penitentiary in Columbus between 1885 and 1963. From 1803, when Ohio became a state, until 1885, executions were carried out by public hanging in the county where the crime was committed.

A Ghoulish History

Downtown Canton's public square and courthouse. *Courtesy of Don Myers.*

One common thread through all of these mentioned hangings is the fact they were all carried out on Friday. In British tradition, Friday was the day of public hangings. Friday executions allegedly date back to the days of ancient Rome.

As you visit downtown Canton in the twenty-first century, pause and reflect a bit as you venture past the courthouse. These streets held thousands of people gathering for public hangings in the 1880s to witness a horrific event. Picnic lunches were said to be sampled on site, and ladies dressed fashionably for the day's proceedings, donning parasols, sun hats and handkerchiefs. Human nature is curious indeed!

THE GREAT INFLUENZA EPIDEMIC OF 1917–18

Not Enough Coffins for Everyone

Imagine a worldwide epidemic that wipes out an estimated twenty to forty million lives. Envision schools closing down, church services halted and panic in the streets. Funeral services can only last a few minutes and sales at local stores are banned due to the risk of contaminating the unaffected souls who might come in for a bargain. Picture entire families affected by death on a daily, if not weekly, basis. To make matters worse, there are not enough coffins for everyone. You now have a snapshot of what it was like to live in 1918. To understand the impact that this deadly virus had on Stark County and the rest of the world, one must be informed of its dark place in medical history. The effect of the influenza epidemic was so severe that the average life span in the United States was depressed by ten years.

The ferocity with which this deadly epidemic struck shocked the general public and healthcare workers alike. We now know that it was caused by an unusually severe and deadly influenza A virus strain of subtype H1N1. This was determined by retrieving tissue samples from a female flu victim buried in the Alaskan permafrost and from samples reserved from American soldiers infected at the time. The flu spread worldwide and even reached remote locations such as the Pacific Islands and the Arctic. The 1918 epidemic has been described as "the greatest medical holocaust in history" and may have killed more people than the Black Death. This strain of influenza virus has been estimated to have killed as many as twenty-five million people in its first twenty-five weeks. Compare those statistics to AIDS, which has claimed twenty-five million in twenty-five years, and you have an idea of the seriousness of this disease. Symptoms in the early days of the outbreak were so unusual that many people were misdiagnosed with dengue, typhoid or cholera. People without symptoms could be stricken suddenly and within hours became too weak to walk, with many dying the next day. Symptoms could include a blue tint to the face and possible coughing up of blood caused by severe obstruction of the lungs. In some more serious cases the virus caused an uncontrollable hemorrhaging that filled the lungs, and patients drowned in their bodily fluids, like those with pneumonia. In other related cases, frequent loss of bowel control would present and the victim would die from losing critical intestinal lining and blood loss. A high fever and general achiness added to the common symptoms many felt.

Any visitor to one of the many Stark County cemeteries may notice common death dates in these local burial grounds. Those years hearken back to a period when words like Belleau Wood, Verdun and Meuse-Argonne were in the daily news as World War I raged overseas. One could surmise that perhaps these burials were a direct result of the fighting overseas, but this could not be farther from the truth. A fight just as real and desperate was occurring on the homefront. It was known as the Influenza Epidemic of 1917–18, and its deadly touch left no family or town unscarred. The epidemic killed more people than World War I.

The influenza epidemic was also known as the Spanish influenza and wreaked havoc across the globe. Ohio was not left unscathed, as thousands perished in the state from this deadly virus. It is thought that the virus actually made its first appearance at a military camp in the United States in March 1918 and did not begin to surface in Spain until May of that year. Spanish influenza was an airborne disease that had no available vaccine. Consequently, it spread easily in the overcrowded conditions of most military camps. The first emergence of the disease in Ohio was in September 1918 at Camp Sherman, a military camp near Chillicothe. The disease swept through the camp in the late summer and early fall. Almost 1,200 men died at Camp Sherman before the epidemic ended. By the end of October 1918, nearly 125,000 cases had been reported in the Buckeye State. In the last week alone, more than 1,500 souls succumbed to the flu and many more continued to fall. One Ohioan who died was the father of former (Ohio) governor Jim Rhodes. Sister Raphael O'Connor, who died just days before her fifty-eighth birthday while nursing influenza victims, was another Ohio casualty. In cities across Ohio, victims succumbed, and cities and towns across the state fell into desperate times.

Hospitals were understaffed and overflowing with the sick. Staffing became an issue in many local hospitals as the employees fell ill alongside their patients. Due to an increasing number of cases, the Red Cross put out many more calls for help and volunteers. Caucasian females were the standard of the nursing profession in 1918, but the agency was now willing to accept volunteers of any race or gender. Canton and Massillon did more than their fair share of recruiting any willing and able-minded woman to help with the cause. Hygiene was taught to many local families, streets and alleys were hosed down with water and swept clean and trash was hauled by these strong ladies of the Red Cross. It was a desperate attempt to curb the spread of the flu.

One building in particular comes to mind when exploring Stark County's experience with the Influenza Epidemic of 1917–18. The former Hercules Engine Factory sits at 1036 Market Street, South, in downtown Canton and once was home to the York Ice Company in the lower level. Built in the 1860s, with manufacturing beginning before the Civil War, this building is just one of several that sit occupying a twenty-six-acre industrial site just south of the downtown area. Ball, Aultman and Co. began making farm implements at the site in 1855 and did so until the Hercules Engine Factory began in 1915. During the height of the flu period, a shortage of coffins was unavoidable. They could not be made quick enough, and even though local furniture stores and cabinet makers tried, they could not keep up with demand. Stories have been told of people simply wrapping up the dead in sheets or quilts and placing them in quickly dug graves. One eyewitness, age twelve at the time, recalls seeing bodies "stacked like cordwood" at a local holding area. Another remembers coffins being stacked up next

Hercules Engine Factory. *Photo by Sherri Brake.*

to a streetlamp for delivery to an unknown destination wrought with death. The Hercules Engine Factory became a holding area as well, with bodies placed on ice in the basement level. What more practical way to keep the dead preserved then using the large blocks of ice stored in the lower level of the factory, which housed the York Ice Company.

The Hercules Engine Factory sits next to the railroad tracks and had a large grassy area next to the building at one time. It was in this grassy area that the city decided to bury the dead it had stored on ice. Some bodies were claimed by family members, but many of the dead were not. Unlucky travelers who came through town and were stricken with the flu were not usually claimed. The homeless, as well as local hobos who had hopped trains into town, were also laid to rest in this grassy spot. Makeshift headstones were constructed, and bodies were laid quickly to rest. During the Second World War, engines were manufactured on site at the factory and shipping and receiving began to take precedence. A new parking lot area for this process was needed immediately. Legend states that headstones and bodies were to be moved to local cemeteries before the lot was paved. Legend also states that this did not take place as methodically as it should have. In other words, bodies were left behind and now lay under pavement with no proper markers.

A Ghoulish History

Inside Hercules Engine Factory.
Photo by Sherri Brake.

To most ghost hunters and paranormal investigators, unmarked graves can lay the groundwork for a typical haunting. People desire to be known in life and also in death. Unmarked graves can sometimes cause a bit of spiritual unrest and can possibly fuel odd and unusual activity. Paranormal activity was often reported by many past factory workers, who spoke of odd sensations, cold spots and fleeting shadows. Some workers even told of equipment malfunctions that would fix themselves mysteriously. A physical presence has been felt by many workers in the past. Sometimes people would report a hand on the shoulder or feelings of being watched while working alone in a remote area. Part of the building actually predates the Civil War, and in this certain area, people have been grabbed or pushed on a stairway. To add to the intrigue of this site, in past years a haunted house held court for the month of October. Very rarely do you run across a haunted house that is actually on the grounds of a location reported by many to be paranormally active. You may wonder what the future holds for this mammoth structure and the other buildings on site. Prospective plans by investors and developers have been in the air since 2005 and include constructing a convention center and office buildings, but as of the writing of this book no changes have taken place to the physical structure of the former Hercules Engine Factory.

The city of Massillon in Stark County fared no better or worse than Canton during the 1918 epidemic. A November 22, 1918 article in the *Massillon Evening Independent* reported a slight decrease in patients as noted by Dr. T. Clarke Miller, city health officer. The number of patients in the Red Cross emergency hospital on North Street in Massillon began diminishing in November 1918. Hospital records show four patients being discharged, with four deaths also occurring in a twenty-four-hour period. Nearby at the Massillon State Psychiatric Hospital on South Erie Street, Dr. Arthur Hyde reported nearly fifty psychiatric patients affected the same week, with three new cases breaking out the last week of November 1918. In the city of Massillon, saloon owners secured a long list of signatures on a petition that asked the local board of health to modify the ban imposed on saloon owners. During the outbreak of the epidemic, saloon owners were asked to limit the hours of operation to help deter the spread of the flu. The saloon owners stated that they did not mind closing their businesses to protect public health, but they also said it was not fair to close their saloons if local shops continued to stay open. The Reverend F.W. Fraser of the Presbyterian church in Massillon, who had been taking an active part in the efforts to slow the epidemic, issued an open letter on November 22, 1918, to the liquor-serving establishments. In Reverend Fraser's letter, he stated that alcohol lowers the body's ability to fight the attack of the influenza germs. Many others, including local doctors and nurses, seemed to think that the saloons contributed greatly to the spread and also pleaded their case to the board of health.

Not enough coffins for everyone. Not enough time for families to say goodbye to loved ones properly and no time for sacred interment for many. Funeral services were scarce, and time was limited for the actual service to take place. Wakes at private homes were practically forbidden as the virus was feared to possibly seek refuge in the living who attended the wake. Fear ran rampant until the virus began to be eradicated in late 1919. For the population of Stark County it not only invoked great panic and fear but also left vacancies at the dinner table and, unfortunately, filled a burial plot for nearly every family in the area.

DINING WITH THE DEAD — SPIRITS ANYONE?

Haunted Taverns and Restaurants

Food so good it's scary? Mixing spirits with spirits? Go ahead and chuckle. There are plenty of ghostly haunts and historical venues throughout the county to visit for food and drink. Benders Tavern in downtown Canton fits the historical bill. Benders is said to be Canton's oldest and finest restaurant, according to its advertisement. It was built in 1889 as the Belmont Building, and Mr. Glen Haliwell opened the Criterion Restaurant at that time. In 1902, it was sold to Mr. Edward Bender and has been in the hands of the Jacobs family for many years now. The atmosphere takes you back to the days of decadence, with marbled décor, tin ceilings and tiger oak–paneled walls. The exterior of the building is Victorian in nature and has aged quite well. Way back in the old days, ladies had a separate entrance to the establishment, as a proper lady would never have been seen in public at a venue that served alcohol. This building also played an important part in local football history, as meetings with the NFL to bring the Professional Football Hall of Fame to Canton took place in an upstairs meeting room in 1962. Is this building haunted? Perhaps not from a ghostly perspective, but one can imagine being transported back in time very easily while sitting here and sampling the fine fare and spirits. Perhaps if you sample more than one beverage you may just see something appear!

The Carriage House at 9033 Columbus Road, Northwest, in Louisville, Ohio, has a long history. It was originally called the Harrisburg Inn and was built in 1816. Located at the intersection

Benders in Canton, 1902. *Photo Courtesy of Benders Restaurant.*

of a crossroads, it was once a popular stagecoach stop and has been rumored to have been a speakeasy and brothel as well. Crossroads are steeped in legend and lore. In the folk magic of many cultures, the crossroads is a location "between the worlds" and, as such, a site where supernatural spirits can be contacted and paranormal events can take place. This is particularly pronounced in conjure, root work and hoodoo, a form of African American magical spirituality. In conjure practice, it is said that in order to achieve great skills, such as playing a musical instrument, throwing dice or dancing, one may visit a crossroads a certain number of times, either at midnight or just before dawn, and there she will meet a "dark man," whom some call the devil, who will bestow upon her the desired skills or abilities. Symbolically, a crossroads can mean a locality where two realms touch and therefore represents liminality, a place literally "neither here nor there."

In downtown Massillon, next to where the Ohio & Erie Canal once flowed, is a restaurant that has stood the test of time. At the time I investigated its alleged paranormal activity it was called Coppers. This investigation took place in December 2003 and was

A carriage house in Louisville. *Photo by Sherri Brake.*

one of the most interesting investigations I have done in Massillon. The building originally housed canal workers on the top floor as they worked on the local canal in the 1820s.

Paranormal activity had been experienced by the majority of the workers I interviewed that day at Coppers. Kitchen workers spoke of food containers moving around mysteriously and many items being lost while showing up in crazy locations later. Upon exploring the second-floor area, I was told by a worker that on several occasions he had seen many of the oven doors open by themselves. He told me that he would step out of the kitchen momentarily and then pop back into the area within a few minutes to find that the bread ovens had opened unexplainably. On the main level, I spoke to one of the nighttime employees who told me she would close up by herself on occasion and would sometimes see shadowy forms moving by the bar area. She then explained to me that these shadowy forms seemed to be full-size men walking on their knees. Of course, that puzzled me and I asked her if she meant that the shadows were dwarflike in size or children and she was very adamant that they had the full-size torsos and arms of men. I interviewed several regulars that day as well and was surprised to find out an interesting fact about the floor. It seems that many years ago during a renovation, it was decided that the floor would need to be built up about ten inches or so. Thinking about the theory that ghosts sometimes walk on the terrain they frequented years ago made me realize a startling fact. These shadowy forms were probably walking on the original floor, which would have been about ten inches lower than the new floor. In other words, they looked as if they were walking on their knees due to the fact that they were walking on a lower floor. Have you ever heard ghost tales told in which the entity walks through a wall? Perhaps back in their time, there was a hallway or a doorway in that location.

Renovations can sometimes stir up activity if you have a location that is paranormally active. Kosmos Grill is now at the old Coppers location at 37 First Street, Southwest, in Massillon. Take time out one evening and go mix spirits with spirits at this more than 150-year-old building. Who knows, maybe you will be lucky enough to see one of the elusive shadow people!

Do you enjoy the towpath and the Ohio & Erie Canal? Do you like the small-town feeling that evokes images of a bygone era? Are you crazy about haunted locations and do you enjoy good food? Meet all of these requirements by stopping by Sisters Century House Restaurant, located in the historic town of Canal Fulton. This building sits on the east side of the Ohio & Erie Canal and is located at 123 South Canal Street. It was built in 1870 and has housed a saloon, general store, private residence and mortuary. That's right, a mortuary. As a matter of fact, Canal Fulton was such a hopping place in the canal era that there were a handful of mortuaries to choose from. This area ran rampant with diseases such as malaria and cholera in the 1830s. Legends along the canal say that there is a dead Irishman for every mile of canal, and perhaps this is why there are so many paranormally active locations that grace the canal way. In this building there have been multiple sightings of ghostly apparitions. A little girl in a white lacey dress has been seen in the upstairs apartment, as well as in the basement area. The story of the little girl in the basement has circulated since the 1970s. A thin man wearing a dark-covered long coat has been seen in this building as well. He would be what I consider a shadow person. Shadow people are a common occurrence, and I would estimate that about 60 percent of people have seen one at one point in their lives.

What is a shadow person or a shadow man? They are shadowlike creatures of both modern folklore and traditional Native American beliefs. In the Appalachian culture I have heard them referred to as "porch people." Most paranormal researchers agree that shadow people are a bit evasive and are typically only seen out of the corner of the eye. As you turn your head to view them, they seem to disappear into thin air. Reports of shadow people occupy a similar position in the popular consciousness to basic ghost sightings but differ slightly. It seems that shadow people are not reported as having human features, wearing modern or

Sisters Century House Restaurant, Canal Fulton. *Photo by Sherri Brake.*

period clothing or attempting to communicate with those who observe them. Shadow forms are not only human, as shadow cats and dogs have been reported as well. Some people believe that shadow people are hallucinations that we can see due to a high electromagnetic field in the area. Our brains are affected by EMFs (electromagnetic fields), which target our temporal region and can alter our perception. Some people believe that shadow people are aliens or ghosts that have a dark energy about them. There are also theories that perhaps shadow people are inter-dimensional and slip back and forth among many dimensions.

At Sisters Century House Restaurant, various workers and visitors have seen or felt paranormal activity on site. In the kitchen, various workers have had unusual things happen to them. Bowls of parsley seem to continually disappear. Pots and pans clank together and then grow still just as quickly as the action began. Near the walk-in pantry in the basement, a woman with long hair and not a single stitch of clothing has been sighted. Some psychics who have visited the site claim that she drowned in the Tuscarawas River while trying to save someone. Near the ice machine in the basement, ghost hunting equipment seems to go haywire. Several workers through the last few years have felt uneasiness in this area. One young lady told me that she would refuse to get her own ice out of the machine, as one time she had her hair pulled and her bottom spanked. On many of our public ghost hunts in this location, we have seen pendulums spin crazily, odd orbs appear in photos and EMF meters spike for no reason whatsoever. If you have the desire to grab a meal at this historic building, tell owners Al and Wendie Berry that you are interested in their ghosts. Bring your appetite... and your camera!

HAUNTED HISTORY
WITH STYLE

Library Ghosts and Haunted Historical Homes

What better place for one to haunt than a library? If I decided to hang around and haunt, I would certainly consider a location like the old Sullivan House in Canal Fulton. Many people know it as the Canal Fulton Public Library, and it stands solidly on the corner of High and Market Streets. Painted a cheery historically correct shade of yellow, this rambling structure beckons you to come inside, pick up a good book and read for a spell. What most patrons do not realize is that this building once housed a mortuary. According to the Ohio Historic Inventory records, this house was built in 1879 and the building contractor was Timothy Sullivan. This was home to Mr. and Mrs. Sullivan, well-to-do and very respected citizens of this quaint canal town. Mr. Sullivan was a grocer and also dealt in building supplies. The site was purchased in 1870 from Israel Harter. After living there for several years, the Sullivans sold the home to E.R. Held, and then in 1901 it was sold to Charles Daily, who operated his undertaking business on the site. In the 1920s, the building was once again sold and in 1949 it became a library. The library had previously been housed at the old high school in town since 1937.

I have interviewed a few employees at the Canal Fulton Public Library over the last sixteen years of my residency in Canal Fulton. Several of the ladies have told me of odd and unusual circumstances occurring on site. One spoke of seeing shadowy figures when no one was present. Another told me she sometimes smelled the odd

Sullivan House/Canal Fulton Public Library. *Courtesy of the Canal Fulton Heritage Society Collection.*

scent of pipe smoke while starting to close up at night. One of the nighttime cleaners spoke of hearing footsteps on the second floor late in the evenings, and on several occasions she would bolt up the steps and check out the area, thinking someone had been trapped in the library overnight. There was an odd anomaly captured by one of the staff of the library several years ago. Renovations had begun, and this staff member snapped some photographs of the progress. Upon reviewing them, she came across an unusual photo. Near the circulation desk was an odd, large, mist-like anomaly. All of the other photos were fine.

Paranormal researchers tag this anomaly as "ectomist." The most basic explanation of ectomist is an anomaly seen on video, film and very rarely with human eyes that is mist-like in form. Ectomist usually displays a swirl effect within a vaporous cloud. There have been numerous photos of this fog or mist from all over the world. In about 75 percent of the photos taken it appears that the usual colors are gray, white or black. Although these mists have also been noted to present in several other colors, white is the most common. Always exercise caution when thinking you have a photo with ectomist. Be sure that no one in the area was smoking a cigarette, cigar or pipe, as smoke can show up in your photo. If you are outdoors, consider the fact that weather conditions can cause mists on film as well. It is important to remember that when trying to capture a mist form, you must take precautions in cold weather because your breath could produce what appears to be ectomist. It will show as a mist form but without the swirl effect in the photo. This would be a false picture in which *nothing* paranormal was captured.

There are many theories about ectomist and what it could represent. Some paranormal investigators believe the mist to be the start of an apparition. There are theories that possibly the mist is the soul or very life essence of a person who has passed. Another theory is that the ectomist is a type of plasma or a collapsed electromagnetic cascade shower. Ectomist and ectoplasm are two different things. Ectoplasm is a physical substance that supposedly manifests as a result of "spiritual energy" or "psychic phenomena." It describes the oozing substance allegedly appearing at many old-time séances, back when Spiritualism was popular. It was often found to be faked by psychics hoping to become famous or make a quick buck.

Another old century home with some paranormal issues can be found in North Canton, not too far from the Hoover Company. This home was built in the early 1900s and is a massive brick building with three floors. The attic area is where most of the paranormal activity tends to happen. I was contacted by the owner in 2001 and a paranormal investigation was requested. The owner had bought the property three years prior and was near the panic stage. He had been experiencing various paranormal activity in the home and was startled on many nights by voices. On another occasion, his young niece saw ghostly children while she was playing up in the attic. The little girl was not alarmed when she saw the other children and continued to play upstairs with the entities. The uncle heard commotion and wondered what his five-year-old niece was doing, since she was alone at play in the shadowy attic area. He checked in on his niece, and when he approached the doorway he noticed that she was standing near a darkened area alone. She was gesturing over her shoulder as she spoke at the vacant attic corner. He paused and took in the scene as his niece continued playing, not knowing that she was being observed. After a few minutes, the uncle became apprehensive and shouted her name.

Odd sounds, footsteps, muffled voices and items moving of their own accord plagued the single owner. One such incident occurred late at night. The owner slept upstairs in a second-floor bedroom and was awakened near midnight by the sound of scraping downstairs. He ran down the oak staircase to find that several of his family photos that had been hanging on the staircase wall were now sitting on the steps of the staircase. Needless to say, he is no longer the owner of this home. He has long since moved on, as he was a bit disturbed at the amount of activity he experienced. I have never been contacted by the new owners and often wonder if they have experienced anything paranormal in the old brick house.

In the Louisville area of the county, I have completed many investigations, and I have always wondered about their proximity to one another. I have investigated a total of five homes on one rambling street that meanders across old farmland. Each of these homes had a common theme of activity, as small children had been seen on site. Not living children mind you, but ghostly children who seemed to be dressed in old-fashioned clothing. Details seemed very sharp with the clothing, as all viewers of these spectral children remembered high-necked collars on the dresses of the little girls and suspenders crossing pale shirts on the little boys. One of the little girls was said to have a white lacy ribbon in her hair. All four families interviewed had multiple family members who had viewed the child ghosts, which tended to appear mostly near dawn hours. The children all appeared in various bedrooms and never in public areas of the homes. The children all tended to be seen standing together in a group and most often at the foot or near the side of the bed.

Why would spectral children appear in various homes on one street? It is possible that this area was once a farm owned by a family with young children. Their ages seemed to be stair-stepped, which means that they were born one or two years apart—a common occurrence back in the old days. Maybe these children fell victim to disease and that's why they are all seen together. Maybe at night they wander on what used to be their farmland and visit the homes, curious about who lives on their property. Ghost hunting is full of theory and conjecture, and in many cases we end up with more questions than answers! Such is the case of the ghostly farm children in Louisville.

In the old Salem Reformed Church in Canal Fulton, there lies some intrigue as well. This building was constructed in 1881 by German immigrants who came to Canal Fulton to work in the local mines during a coal mining strike. It sits on brick-lined High Street in town, near the public library. This building is included on our local nighttime walking tours in Canal Fulton. One question many tour participants ask is what is the Reformed Church faith? Statements of the Reformed Church order that its followers believe that God, since the creation of His world, has been plainly revealed through the things He has made, His eternal power and His divine nature. The faith teaches that the one aim in life and death should be to glorify God and enjoy Him forever. The faith also states that the church is God's spiritual minister for the purpose of redemption and the state is God's providential minister for the purpose of this worldly order.

The Salem Reformed Church building has worn many titles throughout the years. It has housed apartments, a daycare center, a ballet theatre and an arts and crafts store and is now a private home. The proud owners have worked diligently in this home since they purchased it several years ago. The builder of the home was Joshua Bliler, and according to the Ohio Historic Inventory filings, it is Bavarian in architectural style. The red-painted onion dome that tops the home ties in with the building's uniqueness. One of the interesting incidents that took place here involved a worker who had come to do some renovations on the home just purchased by the new owners. The gentleman took out a compass and started to use it inside the home for references on his work. The compass spun off of magnetic north and continued to spin wildly. The worker was, of course, perplexed, to say the least! A compass is the

Salem Reformed Church. *Photo by Sage Recco.*

cheapest piece of investigative equipment that you can purchase. It is thought that paranormal activity can cause a change in polarity or disrupt magnetic fields.

During our nighttime haunted history lantern tours in town, the old Salem Reformed Church has provided us with many great paranormal photos of the outside area of the building. Participants have captured orbs of light around the front of the church and near the steeple area as well. The owners do a fantastic job of decorating the home and the front yard at Halloween time. It is not too often that the front yard of a church has decorations up celebrating the dark holiday we now know as Halloween. This can be evidenced by the amount of people who drive or stroll by during this time of year and stare openly at the fake headstones and creepy characters posed on the old church's yard!

In the town of Massillon, history and hauntings abound. Massillon was named for Bishop Jean-Baptiste Massillon, a clergyman at the French court of Louis XIV. Massillon came into being in the nineteenth century when five villages were joined together. The area thrived when the Ohio & Erie Canal came through in 1828. Massillon became known as the "Port of Massillon," with wheat being its principal export. The town was also a site of steam engine manufacturing in the late 1800s. Other products of Massillon include cigars, glass and coal. Massillon also continued to grow as a center of steel production through the first half of the 1900s. Kendal, now a part of the northeast section of Massillon, was founded in 1812 by Thomas Rotch of Hartford, Connecticut, formerly of Nantucket, Massachusetts. The town of Kendal was

McClymond's mansion, Five Oaks. *Photo by Sherri Brake.*

the first plat to be recorded after Canton became the county seat in 1808. Thomas Rotch had a post office established, and he was appointed postmaster not too long afterward. This town's history is noteworthy in the development of the state of Ohio and is viewed with great pride by its residents. But as with any location steeped in history, there are ghost stories and haunted buildings to explore.

In the historic area of Fourth Street, Northeast, there stand many ornate and beautiful houses. This brick-paved street in Massillon was listed in 1985 on the National Register of Historic Places. One such massive structure on this regal street is the previous home of J. Walter McClymonds and his wife, Flora. The McClymonds were wealthy and respected people in Massillon and built their beautiful family home on the corner of North and Fourth Streets, Northeast. Five Oaks was designed by the noted Cleveland architect Charles F. Schweinfurth, and the home's construction started in 1892. It took several years to complete at the cost of $200,000, and many workers were employed in its construction, including stone masons who sailed from Scotland to work the locally quarried stone on site. Five Oaks was given its name from the fact that there were five oak trees that adorned the landscaped yard. This home's style is a mix of Romanesque and Gothic architecture. This showcase home features an arched portico, large towering chimneys, a corner turret tower, marble fireplaces, a skylight, a billiard room in Moroccan leather, tiffany stained glass, carved stone accents, rare woods and multiple carvings and a modest ballroom located on the third floor. The great hall is most impressive, with its walls in red and green, lavished with fleurs-de-lis and shields stenciled onto the paint in gold leaf. It is truly a history and architecture lover's dream!

As with any old historic building, legends and lore exist and reports of paranormal activity can be heard. This building has a warm, inviting ambience that can be felt the moment you enter through the massive doorway. It is feelings of grandeur and of old days gone by that permeate the atmosphere. But if you are sensitive, or a bit psychic, you may experience something else entirely unexpected. A report of a woman's voice singing in the upstairs area of Five Oaks has been heard. When the singing was investigated, no one could be found on that floor. The smell of pipe or cigar smoke has been noted as well. A woman clothed in a long dress reminiscent of the old days has been seen sitting in the area of the great hall. At a recent nighttime event that we held in the building, a distinct feeling of coldness was experienced in one of the bedrooms upstairs. Cold spots were felt in the grand ballroom, and high EMF readings registered in certain areas on this night of exploring.

Why would someone experience events like this in a grand old building such as Five Oaks? Paranormal researchers believe that ghosts and energy can be tied to a property for various reasons. If you built a grand showplace such as this home, would you not want to stay around for as long as possible? It could be that "Mr. M." is still on site, making sure that his home is treasured and maintained. Paranormal investigators state that whatever personality you have in life carries on in the spirit world. It could be that whoever walks the halls and sings on the second floor is a lover of music and was a guest at one of the many balls held at the mansion many years ago. Perhaps the spectral woman in the dress was a frequent visitor to the home and comes back to see its continued grandeur. There are many reasons why spirits would come back to a certain location. Psychics believe that being tied to the property, stubbornness to not leave the premises, unfinished work or issues with renovations can all be reasons for activity to occur at certain locations. One thing is for certain: if spirits and ghosts wander the halls of Five Oaks at night, they would be greatly pleased to see how well this property has been treated and how it is still a treasure to the locals in Massillon.

GHOSTS ON FILM
AND RADIO

Theatre Haunts, Balcony Ghosts and Radio Station Entities

What better place to haunt then a beautiful theatre? Places such as theatres are filled with the energy of performances past and of the crowd's energy as they clapped in appreciation. The Palace Theatre in Canton is evidence of this very statement. Built in 1926, this venture was a million-dollar project of Harry Harper Ink and housed a vaudeville and movie theatre. Harry Ink was a Canton entrepreneur and industrialist businessman. Harry's ventures also included the Canton-based Tonsiline Company, makers of a cough syrup formula marketed in a unique giraffe-shaped bottle. Harry unfortunately died from cancer before the construction of the theatre was completed. The theatre was designed by the Austrian-born architect John Eberson of Chicago and stands at 605 Market Avenue, North, in downtown Canton.

The Palace Theatre is said to be haunted by several ghosts. In 2005, I interviewed several staff members who were eager to share some of their stories with me. Shadowy forms have been seen moving across a dark and vacant stage. Whispers and muffled voices can be heard from an empty balcony. Disembodied footsteps are heard in the lobby area when no one is around. The ghost of the past organist is said to still "visit" the stage at times, and a ghost of a little girl has been spotted on several occasions, mostly in the upper balcony area. Grab the family and head to the Palace for a movie and some popcorn, but don't be surprised if you see more than you bargained for!

The Palace Theatre. *Photo by Sherri Brake.*

A Ghoulish History

WHBC Studio. *Photo by Sherri Brake.*

WHBC radio station is the oldest radio station in Canton. It is located at 550 Market Avenue, South. The license for the station was granted on February 13, 1925, to Father Edward P. Graham and the St. John Catholic Church. WHBC began broadcasting on March 9, 1925, and continues to this very day. The station has a bit of an unusual history, as a shadowy form has been seen lurking in the halls. A newsman was tragically killed out in front of the station when he was hit by a car many years ago. Perhaps he still has unfinished business here.

I have done several radio shows with host Ron Ponder. Most of the shows take place on Halloween morning, and it never ceases to amaze me what quirky little things happen while on site. One year, all of the phone calls were mysteriously disconnected while on hold. Another broadcast had us in the studio as a few lights went on and off. It was then that I noticed that the station number 1480 added up to the number 13.

STARK FRIGHTS

Haunts in the Hospital and Apparitions in the Asylum

Why would paranormal activity occur in hospitals and asylums? If energy is the basis for all hauntings, think what type of energy would be left in these buildings. In hospitals you typically have the joy of birth, the sadness of death, the grief of families who are mourning a new loss, the anxiousness of patients before surgery and the fear of treatments and procedures. This energy is thought to sometimes be left behind and is called residual or imprinted energy by paranormal investigators. A residual haunting is a playback of a past event. The apparitions involved are not spirits; rather, they are "recordings" of the event. The easiest way to explain this type of haunting is to compare it to an old film loop, meaning that it is a scene or image that is played over and over again through the years. Many of the locations in which these hauntings take place experience an event, or a series of events, that imprints itself on the atmosphere of a place. This event can suddenly discharge and play itself at various times. The events are not always visual, but they are often replayed as sounds and noises that have no explanation. The famous "phantom footsteps" reported in many haunted places are a perfect example of this.

To understand the possible haunting of a location, the history of that spot should be explored. In Massillon, on a hilltop east of Route 21, sit a few old vacant buildings. This land was originally settled by James Duncan, who arrived in 1816 from Portsmouth, New Hampshire. Duncan grazed sheep on the "plains," formerly

The Massillon State Psychiatric Hospital with water tower. *Photo Courtesy of the Karen Kline Collection.*

the cornfields of the local Native Americans. This land is now occupied by the old Massillon State Hospital, and the original cottage was used as a dwelling until 1956. Approximately 240 acres of this land were given to the state by the citizens of Massillon at the suggestion of William McKinley while he was governor. The hospital was ready for its first patients in 1898 (it was also Massillon State Hospital for the Insane at the time). Under the supervision of the building board, a dining room building, a kitchen and bakery building, a storehouse, a boiler house, a power house, a carpenter shop, a laundry building, a hospital building, an infirmary building, a superintendent's residence, a steward's residence and seven cottages were constructed. Nearly forty buildings sat on the property of the hospital. The facility had its own power station and water tower, and trolley cars would run from town to the hospital on a daily basis.

The population of the hospital grew quickly, and in 1950 it had three thousand residents. With the growth of the patient population, disease spread and many succumbed to death's grip. If no family

A Ghoulish History

An old postcard with the superintendent's house, Massillon State Hospital.
Postcard Courtesy of the Karen Kline Collection.

member claimed the deceased, the body was placed in Potter's Field at the Massillon cemetery on Erie Street. A special section was provided for those who could not afford a proper burial spot and had no funds. It is estimated that over one hundred Massillon State patients lie at rest in the Massillon cemetery. Many do not have headstones or markers of any sort, and some are even buried on top of each other to conserve space.

One of the buildings that is reportedly the most active is the old McKinley Hall. This fifty-two-thousand-square-foot brick building has an imposing feel on approach. McKinley Hall served as hospital administration, a nurse's dormitory and a commissary. Sightings of a small boy in a ball hat have been shared with me through various interviews. The small boy was sighted by several nurses who stayed in the dorms, as well as a past utility worker. On a 2005 Haunted Heartland bus trip to the hospital site, a local reporter and photographer caught a blurry image of what looks like the little boy in one of their photos. One of the nurses I interviewed stated that many ladies had seen the little boy darting down the hallways in McKinley Hall, mostly in the evenings. Children were patients in this facility along with teens and adults. Is this the ghost of a little boy who still plays a spectral game of tag or hide-and-

McKinley Hall, Massillon State Hospital (built in 1901). *Photo by Sherri Brake.*

seek? Or perhaps it is just the over-active imagination of workers stuck on the graveyard shift in an eerie hospital.

Another location in Massillon that has a ghostly past is the now closed Doctors Hospital. The hospital changed hands a few years ago and finally closed its doors in 2008, but not before it left its tale in haunted history. One room located on the first floor has had paranormal activity for many years. This room finally ended up being closed as a patient room and was used specifically as storage. Many patients through the years complained of shadows moving eerily in the room. When the room was empty, nurses and aides noticed the call light coming on by itself, as if some ghostly form needed assistance getting out of bed. Doctors Hospital is mentioned as a haunted location in Chris Woodyard's excellent series on ghosts in Ohio. *Haunted Ohio* is a wonderful resource for those interested in the spooky Buckeye State.

Molly Stark Sanitarium stands north of the town of Louisville, Ohio, and has quite an interesting past. Located at 7900 Columbus Road, Northeast, and sitting on forty-three acres, it may soon

A Ghoulish History

Molly Stark Sanitarium. *Photo by Mike and Melanie Warner.*

be demolished and banished to the annals of history books. It currently stands with towering brick walks, ornate marble, chandeliers and stone decorations. Arson in the past has scorched and scarred its interior and ghostly legends mar its history. It served as a tuberculosis sanitarium, opening in 1929, and later becoming a state hospital for the mentally ill and the aged. Molly Stark was the wife of Revolutionary War general John Stark. Molly passed away in 1814 and was the mother of eleven children.

The old hospital still possesses a great appeal to those of us interested in architecture and design. The architect, Albert L. Thayer of Pennsylvania, used numerous rooftop porches and loggia or arched galleries. The rooftop porches on this structure were originally used as spaces where patients could sit outside, covered in blankets, to take in the fresh air. Fresh air and sunlight were thought to help cure tuberculosis, or the white plague as some

Molly Stark Sanitarium. *Photo Courtesy of the Mike Allen Collection.*

called it. The main building housed 128 beds, and the children were housed separately in a 38-bed structure.

Paranormal activity has been reported throughout the years and even during the days of operation. Several nurses have told of elevators that would run by themselves and shadowy apparitions seen down long empty hallways. Glowing lights have been seen inside this building since it closed in 1995.

The building and property were closed in 1995 by county commissioners and the state cut off funding. Asbestos worries (totaling $2 million in removal cost), lead paint and structural issues have caused problems since the closing of the site in the mid-1990s. Over the past years it has been considered as a site for a county park, a school and also a fire station. None of these have materialized, and it appears that it may be headed for a date with a wrecking ball. As of the writing of this book, Molly Stark Sanitarium still stands silent and waiting for its fate to be decided.

DOWSING FOR GRAVES

Unmarked Graves, Ancient Burials and the Forgotten Dead

What is it about old graveyards that tends to frighten many of the living and intrigue others? Is it the eerie quietness of the silent city? Is it the spooky remoteness of old rural cemeteries that causes concern? Perhaps it's the innate fear that we are not alone as we stroll along the soldier-like rows of headstones, crypts and mausoleums. Hollywood has done its best to feed our fear of cemeteries and the dead. It's a natural fear and one that has been prevalent throughout time. Whatever the reason, many of us fear death, the dead and places of burial.

Ancient people marked graves with rocks and stones, which they piled on top of the freshly buried corpses. These ancient markers were not meant to alert others to final burial spots but to prevent the dead from rising up and out of their graves and haunting the living. It is believed that the Neanderthals were the first to hold funeral services. We know by uncovering some of these ancient sites that they had specific ways of burying their dead. Many were laid out in the east–west direction to correspond with the rising and setting of the sun. Others were laid out in the fetal position, as if they were still in the womb. In many ancient burial sites there is a high amount of pollen, suggesting that flowers may have been laid in the grave. Radio carbon testing at archaeological sites across the world has dated various burial sites back to 70,000 BCE. The earliest undisputed burial dates back 130,000 years. Human skeletal remains stained with red ochre were discovered in the Skhul Cave at Qafzeh, Israel. A variety of grave goods were present at the site, including the mandible of a wild boar in the arms of one of the skeletons.

The act of seeing our deceased off into the afterlife is a trait that runs through most civilizations. *Encyclopedia Britannica* defines the beginning of civilization itself as when we first started to bury our dead:

> *It is the definition of the anthropologist that, in the evolution from ape-like kindred species, civilized man began to exist when he first buried his dead. This is the definition of homo sapiens—wise man—rational man—thinking man.*

Ancient people living in Mesopotamia believed that death was miserable. If you died, it meant a grim existence in *ku-nu-gi-a*, or the land of no return, where dead people live in darkness, eat clay and are clothed like birds with wings. Dead people were feared in most cultures. The Shawnee tribe in America called the dead *ahsanwah*, which meant "vanished" or "disappeared." The Shawnees believed that they needed to offer plates of food on a daily basis to placate their dead family members. The Chippewa tribe also believed in offering food to the departed to keep them appeased.

Not all cultures believed in fearing the dead. The ancient Egyptians had a very different approach. They believed that people's fates after death depended on how they lived their lives. The ancient Egyptians paid a great deal of attention to death and developed elaborate rituals to help ensure a happy afterlife. The Egyptians were so preoccupied with death that they sometimes spent years preparing for it. Egyptian mummification would sometimes take as long as seventy days to complete.

During the Viking era, from 789 to 1066 CE, we can see many ideas from ancient Egypt carried through to Viking burial. Vikings were pagan in their beliefs and viewed gods and spirits as entities to call upon when needed. The typical Viking warrior would be buried with some of his belongings, such as his weapons and his shield. On occasion, a favorite animal or horse might be killed to accompany the dead Viking on his travels through the afterlife.

A Ghoulish History

In many cultures, human corpses were usually buried in soil. The act of burying corpses is thought to have begun about 200,000 years ago during the Paleolithic period before spreading out from Africa. As a result, burial grounds are found throughout the world. Mounds of earth, temples and underground caverns were used to store the dead bodies of ancestors. In modern times, the custom of burying dead people below ground with a stone marker to mark the grave is used in almost every modern culture, although other means, such as cremation, are becoming more popular in the West (cremation is the norm in India and mandatory in Japan). Some burial practices are heavily ritualized, while others are simply practical and done without ceremony.

The Great Plains Indians of the western United States felt that the earth's soil was too sacred for the dead to be placed into. They would dress their dead in their best clothing and place them in the fork of a tree, where the birds of prey could pick the bones clean. Once the birds had feasted and the white bones were picked clean, the skeletons would be gathered and then interred in the soil.

Across time and traversing the entire world, we have been marking graves in various ways. In any cemetery in America you may see recumbent markers, upright markers, various Christian crosses, Celtic crosses, mausoleums, statuary, angels with swords, books and garlands and various other markers of the dead. Entire books have been written on the subject of cemetery symbolism and grave styles. It's a matter of personal style, religion and cultural beliefs as to how one marks the grave of their families and loved ones. The dead may be placed in a number of different positions. In Christian burials, the dead lie flat, with arms and legs straight or with the arms folded on the chest. Extended burials may be done with the body lying on the front. In some cultures however, being buried facedown shows disrespect. Other ritual practices place the body in a flexed position, with the legs bent or crouched, folded up to the chest. Warriors in some ancient societies or tribes were buried in an upright position. In Islam, the head is pointed toward and the face is turned toward Mecca, the holiest city in Islam. Many cultures treat placement of dead people in an appropriate position to be a sign of respect, even when burial is impossible.

Burial procedures through the years have ranged from primitive and simple to the very ornate and almost decadent. Burials during plagues and epidemics were coarse and crude at best. The inflicted were hauled onto carts and wagons and taken to central areas where large fires had been lit. Many times religious ceremonies were neglected during times such as these, and no proper words or blessings were uttered. Burial protocol was overlooked, as the living took precedence over the dead during plagues. Some cultures would wrap the deceased in funeral shrouds of simple white cotton, while others would use vibrant shades of color and expensive fabric such as silk or satin. There are world cultures that demand that bodies be buried immediately after death, while other religions and cultures prefer a waiting period of three or even seven days before the bodies are buried. Many religions insist on cremation of the earthly body, while others deem cremation a sin. Ancient tribes sometimes insisted on building upright wooden structures that would hold the dead in the air on a sort of platform, enabling the souls to reach heaven more easily. Worldwide opinion on how to bury the dead has always varied and continues to do so today as we have entered the twenty-first century.

Marking the graves of the dead was customary in all of America, but there were certain circumstances in which proper marking could not be done for various reasons. These reasons could stem from the simple fact that a stone was never purchased by the family, due to monetary reasons, simple neglect or even the fact that family members moved out of the area or died before stones could be purchased. Other reasons could include the influenza outbreak in 1917–18 and various cholera epidemics that swept across Ohio. The most devastating cholera outbreak in Ohio was in the year 1849. These periods of plague left little time for many to be buried properly, as official funeral services were not permitted due to the contagious nature of the viruses or diseases.

In Stark County, we have many cemeteries that have deemed certain areas as Potter's Field or Pauper's Field. These areas are often not marked with signs telling you this fact, but usually the cemetery office or association will show you or hand you a cemetery map if you are curious. The term *Potter's Field* probably derives from the Gospel of Matthew in the Christian Bible. In the Book of Matthew, after Judas Iscariot betrays Christ, he repents and returns his payment of thirty pieces of silver to the priests before hanging himself. The priests called the coins "the price of blood" and did not want to put them in the temple treasury, so they used them to buy a field: "And they took counsel, and bought with them the potter's field, to bury strangers in." The Bible then records Judas as saying:

> *"I have sinned in betraying innocent blood." But they said: "What is that to us? Look thou to it." And casting down the pieces of silver in the temple, he departed, and went and hanged himself with a halter. But the chief priests, having taken the pieces of silver, said: "It is not lawful to put them into the corbona, because it is the price of blood." And after they had consulted together, they bought with them the potter's field, to be a burying place for strangers. For this the field was called Haceldama, that is, the field of blood, even to this day.*

Heading south on Erie Street in Massillon, located a few miles down the road from the Massillon cemetery was the Massillon State Psychiatric Hospital. Quite a few of the graves in Potter's Field are filled with patients from this state-run facility. If the patient's family did not claim the body or pay for a regular burial spot, the afflicted would end up here. Bodies in this area may also be placed double-decker style; in other words, placed with two caskets on top of each other as a way to save funds and possibly conserve space as well. Standing in the Potter's Field area and facing west toward Route 21, you will notice a steep hillside leading down to the highway. There are multiple graves placed here as well, and I am sure that travelers on Route 21 north have no idea what lies on that wooded hillside as they speed past en route to their destinations.

Plum Street Cemetery in downtown Canton is another example of a cemetery long forgotten. This cemetery was designated as Canton's first cemetery in 1805 by its founder, Bezaleel Wells. Mr. Wells purchased land from the United States government in 1805 and began to plat the new village he named Canton. One of the areas on the original plat map was designated as a cemetery. Plum

The Potter's Field hillside in the Massillon cemetery. *Photo by Sherri Brake.*

Street Cemetery was originally located on the outskirts of town but quickly became full and outgrew its designated boundaries. It was platted on Sixth Street and McKinley Avenue, Southwest, which was originally called Plum Street. Approximately "336 loads of earth carried in by wagons" were said to have been placed in this area, according to a Canton City Board of Commissioners report in 1897. The first burial in this cemetery is said to have been that of the wife of Butcher John Matthews and occurred in the spring of 1808. She had died as a result of childbirth, which was a common cause of death in early times. Mrs. Matthews's child was said to be the first "white" child born in the city limits of the newly established town of Canton. The second interment was that of Blacksmith John Bouer (Bower). He fell victim to death's cruel hand in June 1808. For such a simple cemetery, it was in the public eye the day that President McKinley gave a speech from a temporarily erected grandstand behind a row of headstones. Plum Street Cemetery eventually became known as McKinley Cemetery at a later date.

As the cemetery filled, it was announced that all bodies but one were to be removed for burial elsewhere. Bezaleel Wells, the founder

The lone grave of Mr. Kline in the old Plum Street Cemetery. *Photo by Sherri Brake.*

of Canton, deeded this land to the city for use as a cemetery. If the cemetery was moved completely, there was a chance that a descendant of Mr. Wells could legally claim the property and the city would lose its rights to the land. One stone remains standing, offering testament to the fact that this was Canton's first official cemetery. In 1897, the city council issued an order to Mr. Francis Reed, park superintendent, asking him to lay down the tombstones then standing in Plum Street Cemetery. The inscriptions were to lie face up, and all stones were to be covered with earth and sown grass seed. All but several stones were said to be covered, and only one stands this very day. The gravestone of Mr. Obed H. Kline, who died of consumption March 8, 1845, stands near the center of the block. Mr. Kline was thirty-one years old. There have been said to be nearly two hundred graves at Plum Street Cemetery, but no one knows for sure.

It is a bit peculiar to stand on this raised block of land and realize that children play on the playground equipment and couples stroll the sidewalk across forgotten graves of the dead. Rumor has it that when local street and sewer projects were undertaken, skeletons were found when digging where many bodies were believe to have been already removed. Whether from human error or neglect, we may never know, but many paranormal researchers will surmise that paranormal activity happens where graves are not marked properly.

There is a curious story about one headstone that stands today in the basement area under Canton's Diebold Plant Number 1. The plant opened in the 1872 and was built in a former cemetery located at 818 Mulberry Road and Madison Avenue, Southeast, in Canton. As with all old cemeteries, bodies and stones were to be removed and relocated, but in this instance, one was left behind. Sounds like a Hollywood movie, right? Avarilla Ann married Richard Vandegrift on August 10, 1832, and they settled on eighty-five acres of farmland that he had purchased locally. Richard and Avarilla were first cousins. This may sound strange in today's society, but cousins married often back in the old days. Avarilla was the daughter of Edward and Cassandra Courtney. According to county cemetery records, the Vandergrift couple had four children:

A Ghoulish History

Edward, Jefferson, Robert and Lydia. Avarilla was forty-five years old when she passed from this life. Her cause of death is not known, as death certificates were not required in Ohio until 1867. Avarilla passed away on May 4, 1857. (She was born in 1812.) She had lived a long life—forty-five was considered to be the normal life span at that time.

When the old cemetery was to be moved, Avarilla's parents and her husband's body were removed to the Hawkins Family Cemetery in Washington Township, Stark County. And now the mystery! Her lone tombstone sits in the basement of Diebold Plant Number 1. There is a rumor that a state code exists deeming that one grave was to be left behind when cemeteries were moved. Is this the case with Avarilla Ann? Her stone leans against a sturdy column in the basement area and causes speculation of whether she is buried under the foundation. Employees call it "Tombstone at Plant No. 1." The room it is stored in is otherwise empty and at one time housed records for the corporation. Odd occurrences have happened around her tombstone. Some employees claim they have smelled the scent of rose perfume. It is hoped that her body was removed from the old cemetery and lies buried in an unmarked grave, resting next to her husband Richard in the Hawkins Family Cemetery. We may never know for sure.

In the case of unmarked graves, there are basically three general ways to locate bodies. The most invasive method would be to simply dig the up body. Of course this would be expensive and require legal action. A noninvasive means of locating bodies would be the use of ground-penetrating radar or GPR. This is an expensive method that can locate utilities, storage tanks, sink holes, water tables, buried artifacts, land mines and graves. GPR works by emitting a series of FCC-approved high-frequency, high-amplitude electromagnetic pulses (radio waves) that reflect off of underground irregularities. The resulting digital GPR data is fed into a portable video display, which provides a real-time "picture" of a slice of the subsurface area in question. GPR is high tech and expensive. A second, more feasible, method to locate graves, both unmarked and marked, would be by the use of dowsing or divining rods.

Dowsing rods have been used for thousands of years to locate items that are lost or desired. In fourteenth-century France, they were used to locate silver for mining. Underground water sources, land mines, water and electrical lines, tunnels and graves are just a few of the ways that dowsing can be applied. The word *dowse* is defined in *Webster's Dictionary* as meaning "to seek or to find." There are two types of rod styles: L rods and Y rods. Y rods are more commonly used for water dowsing or water witching. Y rods can be made from a variety of materials, with wood being the material of choice for many water dowsers. Tree limbs that fork into a Y are commonly cut and used for a period of three or four days for dowsing and then discarded. Hazel wood or witch hazel is preferred by many water dowsers. A leading theory associates witch hazel with water dowsing or divining. It became the shrub or tree of choice for obtaining forked limbs for water dowsing, so it is thought that the name became attached to the shrub because of its use by water witches in detecting groundwater. The idea that witch hazel limbs could be used to find groundwater may have begun with the Mohegan Indians, and white immigrants observed its use. *Wicke* is Middle English for "lively" and *wych* is an old Anglo-Saxon word for "bend." The shrub may have been dubbed a wicke hazel by the pilgrims because the dowsing end of the forked dowsing limb became "lively" and bent downward when the dowser carried it over ground with water beneath.

L rods are L-shaped rods. You grasp the short ends, one in each hand, as you hold the long length of the rod parallel to the ground. Materials used in L rods could be copper, brass, chrome or even plain old-fashioned metal clothes hangers. Some dowsers prefer to have wooden dowels or plastic sleeves placed on the handles of the rods to impede any conscious movement of the hand while dowsing. Others find that this allows too much movement of the rod. It is simply up to the dowser to find what works for him or her by trial and error. Practice is most important with dowsing, as the more you dowse, the more it will come easily to you.

Most cemeteries in the United States bury their dead in a Christian manner. What this basically means is that all bodies are laid with the head pointing west and the feet pointing east. In newer cemeteries, the east–west orientation has fallen to the wayside, as cemetery road placement mandates the positioning of new burials and space is a precious commodity when placing final resting spots. If you travel to the New England area, be sure to note some of the grave placements in the older cemeteries. If one was accused of practicing witchcraft, the grave placement was usually in a north–south orientation so as not to allow the deceased possible entrance to the heavens above.

When trying to locate a lost cemetery or dowse graves, it is best to walk in north–south direction in order to pick up a pattern. Usually you will find the graves to be separated by two to three feet. As you cross each grave, the rods will cross and then uncross as you step off of the grave. I find that I take two to three steps between each grave. If you find that a pattern develops (cross, three steps, cross, three steps, etc.), you have most likely found a cemetery. You will then need to determine the perimeter of the cemetery. By walking north and south, you can come close to determining where the burials begin and end. When you reach the edges of the burial ground and are no longer picking up bodies, go back to the last grave and begin walking east and west. You will now be picking up on the length of the body, you will get some variances depending on whether infants, children or adults occupy the end graves. Keep walking east and west until you are no longer picking up bodies. By the time you have completed a square, you will have a good idea of the perimeters of the cemetery. Be sure to always check past the last body for at least twenty feet. Remember that you are looking for a pattern. You will find that Christian burial grounds are very well laid out. Usually the graves will be side by side and head to toe in perfectly straight lines.

To find graves while using L rods to dowse, you simply hold two rods in your hands with your arms comfortably flexed, as if holding two pistols. Keep the rods level and out in front of you as you walk the area in question. Concentration is important, so be sure to concentrate on what it is you desire to find. To locate a body, simply walk the area and think or say "Body, body, body." Once you have walked or stepped onto an area where there is a body buried, the two dowsing rods will begin to move toward each other and eventually will cross over top of each other. This signifies a positive response. In other words, your target has been found. It is estimated that nearly 80 percent of people have this ability. Science tends to scoff at dowsing, and it does not have a plausible reason as to why it may work. Dowsing has been the redheaded step child of science for many years and until solid proof can be had, it will remain that way. Over the last twelve years I have dowsed with great success and have instructed thousands of people who have repeatedly had success with their own dowsing adventures. It always delights me to see someone's face light up when they discover they have this natural ability. I have noticed that there are a few working professionals who may struggle initially with dowsing. Engineers, CPAs and bank employees, or those who deal with numbers or analysis, tend to have issues with dowsing. It has been said that while dowsing, the right side and left side of the brain work in sync with each other.

All in all, dowsing continues to be a controversial procedure and also defies any scientific explanation. On many occasions, I have been asked to help local land developers, historical societies and cemetery associations in the area of finding possible unmarked graves. The recent explosion of interest in the paranormal has taken dowsing to a whole new level. Many of my dowsing students contact me with wonderful stories of finding unmarked graves in old cemeteries or of using the dowsing rods to find lost objects. I always encourage people to have an open mind and to just give it a try!

GOT GHOSTS?

How to Investigate What Goes Bump in the Night

Apparitions, ghosts, specters, phantoms, spooks and wraiths—various words that all basically describe an entity of paranormal phenomena. Since the beginning of time, mankind has speculated, theorized and pondered on that which is ghostly or paranormal. The word *geist* is Germanic in origin and does not translate very well into English, but essentially it means "spirit" or "ghost." Another popular word heard in paranormal circles is poltergeist. *Poltergeist* is German and means "noisy ghost"; generally, it is used in reference to collective energy. *Ghost* is by far the most common word in the paranormal vocabulary and can encompass a multitude of phenomena. Ghosts and spirits have been documented as far back as the start of time, with inclusion in several passages in the Christian Bible:

> *Luke 24:39: Handle me and see, because a spirit does not have flesh and bones, as you see me having.*

> *Mark 16:12: To two of them, as they are going into a field, walking, he was manifested in another form.*

> *Matthew 14:26: And the disciples having seen him walking upon the sea were troubled saying, "It is an apparition," and from the fear they cried out.*

Methods of investigating the paranormal vary from person to person. Investigators can take a multitude of approaches. Some investigators take a more psychic approach and rely on intuitive feelings and metaphysical equipment such as dowsing rods and pendulums. Other investigators apply a more scientific approach and implement the use of various scientific equipment such as electromagnetic field detectors, night vision binoculars, motion detectors, ion counters and digital voice recorders. Paranormal investigators can employ the use of various cameras, including SLR, digital and video cameras that feature night vision. There are also investigators who prefer to use no equipment whatsoever and basically live for the moment during the investigation.

The paranormal field has grown by leaps and bounds since the year 2000, partially due to the explosion of paranormally themed television shows. Evidence of the interest in the paranormal is plainly seen on the World Wide Web, with the multitude of web radio shows on ghosts and the growth of ghost hunting as a hobby in general. In the state of Ohio alone, there have been as many as 210 recorded ghost hunting groups and paranormal investigators. This list was compiled starting in 2008, leading up to the publication of this book. Brian Fain, founder of the Massillon Ghost Hunters Society, has taken on the job of compiling the list of ever-growing groups in the Buckeye State with the hopes of establishing a database for paranormal groups (www.massillonghosthunters.com).

What has fueled the recent increased interest in the paranormal? I believe it is due to several factors: the human psyche and its search for the unknown, the acceptance of the paranormal as a hobby and the general increase in people attaining spiritual growth. Since the new millennium, various publishers have noticed a huge increase in the sale of books by popular psychics, as well as books dealing with the metaphysical aspects of life. On a more private note, and since starting my own haunted history tour company in 2004, I have seen an increase in attendance from year to year. I sometimes ask participants their reasons for attending a ghost hunt and their answers differ greatly. Many times they attend out of curiosity, and other times it is due to the fact that they want to investigate or join up with a group of like-minded individuals.

A Ghoulish History

How does one begin to investigate the paranormal? Too many times beginners want to start out by purchasing expensive items and are surprised that it can be done at a reasonable cost. You do not need to purchase every piece of ghost hunting gear out there. Buy what you can afford and most of all learn to use it properly. If you buy a camera, learn its limits, explore the various settings and be sure you know how to maintain it. The biggest mistake I see among investigators armed with cameras is that they do not take the time to keep the camera lens clean and they forget to bring extra batteries on investigations and ghost hunts. Get yourself a digital tape recorder and try your hand at recording electronic voice phenomena. Grab a 35 millimeter or digital camera. Read every book you can on the subject and get out there and explore!

There are a multitude of paranormal organizations across the world. If you are interested in joining a group be sure that they have protocol and procedures for investigating. A good investigative group is responsible and respectful of properties investigated and people interviewed. They will acquire permission to investigate a location and will never ever trespass.

Enjoy your pursuit of the paranormal and of the history of this area of northeast Ohio. Join the local genealogical society or historical society or volunteer to clean up at a local cemetery. But above all, be respectful of cemeteries, old historical buildings and those who have passed on to the great beyond.

Stop by here my friends
As you pass by;
As you are now
So once was I.
As I am now
So you must be.
Prepare for death
And follow me.
—*Old Grave Epitaph*

ABOUT THE AUTHOR

S herri Brake has been a resident of Stark County, Ohio, for over forty years. Her love of the paranormal and history in general led her to begin her own company, Haunted Heartland Tours (www.hauntedhistory.net), in 2004. She is a member of various heritage, historical and paranormal organizations and is the mother of two children, Sage and Mason Recco.

Visit us at
www.historypress.net

www.ingramcontent.com/pod-product-compliance
Lightning Source LLC
Chambersburg PA
CBHW060752100426
42813CB00004B/782